Oversharing: Presentations of Self in the Internet Age

Ben Agger

D1360728

People "overshare" when they interact with others through the screens of computers and smartphones. Oversharing means to divulge more of their inner feelings, opinions, and sexuality than they would in person, or even over the phone. Text messaging, Facebooking, tweeting, camming, blogging, online dating, and Internet porn are vehicles of this oversharing, which blurs the boundary between public and private life. This book examines these "presentations of self," acknowledging that we are much more public about what used to be private. The book concludes with reflections on the impact of oversharing on identity, friendship, sexuality, family, and democracy, and suggests steps people can take to re-establish the boundary between public and personal life.

Ben Agger is Professor of Sociology and Humanities and Director of the Center for Theory at the University of Texas at Arlington. He works in critical theory and media/cultural studies. Among his recent books are *Body Problems: Running and Living Long in a Fast-Food Society* and, with Tim Luke, *A Journal of No Illusions: Telos, Paul Piccone and the Americanization of Critical Theory*. He edits the journal *Fast Capitalism*, which can be found at www.fastcapitalism.com.

 **University Readers** Reading Materials Evolved.   **THE SOCIAL ISSUES COLLECTION**    **Routledge** Taylor & Francis Group

Framing 21st Century Social Issues

The goal of this new, unique Series is to offer readable, teachable "thinking frames" on today's social problems and social issues by leading scholars. These are available for view on http://routledge.customgateway.com/routledge-social-issues.html.

For instructors teaching a wide range of courses in the social sciences, the Routledge *Social Issues Collection* now offers the best of both worlds: originally written short texts that provide "overviews" to important social issues *as well as* teachable excerpts from larger works previously published by Routledge and other presses.

As an instructor, click to the website to view the library and decide how to build your custom anthology and which thinking frames to assign. Students can choose to receive the assigned materials in print and/or electronic formats at an affordable price.

Available

Body Problems
Running and Living Long in a Fast-Food Society
Ben Agger

Sex, Drugs, and Death
Addressing Youth Problems in American Society
Tammy Anderson

The Stupidity Epidemic
Worrying About Students, Schools, and America's Future
Joel Best

Empire Versus Democracy
The Triumph of Corporate and Military Power
Carl Boggs

Contentious Identities
Ethnic, Religious, and Nationalist Conflicts in Today's World
Daniel Chirot

The Future of Higher Education
Dan Clawson and Max Page

Waste and Consumption
Capitalism, the Environment, and the Life of Things
Simonetta Falasca-Zamponi

Rapid Climate Change
Causes, Consequences, and Solutions
Scott G. McNall

The Problem of Emotions in Societies
Jonathan H. Turner

Outsourcing the Womb
Race, Class, and Gestational Surrogacy in a Global Market
France Winddance Twine

Changing Times for Black Professionals
Adia Harvey Wingfield

Forthcoming

Oversharing: Presentations of Self in the Internet Age

Ben Agger

University of Texas at Arlington

Routledge
Taylor & Francis Group

NEW YORK AND LONDON

First published 2012
by Routledge
711 Third Avenue, New York, NY 10017

Simultaneously published in the UK
by Routledge
2 Park Square, Milton Park, Abingdon, Oxon OX14 4RN

Routledge is an imprint of the Taylor & Francis Group, an informa business

Library of Congress Cataloging in Publication Data
Agger, Ben.
    Oversharing : presentations of self in the Internet age / Ben Agger.
    p. cm. — (Framing 21st century social issues)
    1. Internet—Social aspects. 2. Online identities. 3. Self-presentation. 4. Identity (Psychology) 5. Discretion. 6. Information society. I. Title.
    HM851.A335 2011
    302.23'1—dc23
    2011039702

ISBN13: 978-0-415-50912-1 (pbk)
ISBN13: 978-0-203-12509-0 (ebk)

Typeset in Garamond and Gill Sans
by EvS Communication Networx, Inc.

University Readers (www.universityreaders.com): Since 1992, University Readers has been a leading custom publishing service, providing reasonably priced, copyright-cleared, course packs, custom textbooks, and custom publishing services in print and digital formats to thousands of professors nationwide. The Routledge Custom Gateway provides easy access to thousands of readings from hundreds of books and articles via an online library. The partnership of University Readers and Routledge brings custom publishing expertise and deep academic content together to help professors create perfect course materials that are affordable for students.

Printed and bound in the United States of America by Publishers Graphics, LLC on sustainably sourced paper.

Contents

Series Foreword

The world in the early 21st century is beset with problems—a troubled economy, global warming, oil spills, religious and national conflict, poverty, HIV, health problems associated with sedentary lifestyles. Virtually no nation is exempt, and everyone, even in affluent countries, feels the impact of these global issues.

Since its inception in the 19th century, sociology has been the academic discipline dedicated to analyzing social problems. It is still so today. Sociologists offer not only diagnoses; they glimpse solutions, which they then offer to policy makers and citizens who work for a better world. Sociology played a major role in the civil rights movement during the 1960s in helping us to understand racial inequalities and prejudice, and it can play a major role today as we grapple with old and new issues.

This series builds on the giants of sociology, such as Weber, Durkheim, Marx, Parsons, Mills. It uses their frames, and newer ones, to focus on particular issues of contemporary concern. These books are about the nuts and bolts of social problems, but they are equally about the frames through which we analyze these problems. It is clear by now that there is no single correct way to view the world, but only paradigms, models, which function as lenses through which we peer. For example, in analyzing oil spills and environmental pollution, we can use a frame that views such outcomes as unfortunate results of a reasonable effort to harvest fossil fuels. "Drill, baby, drill" sometimes involves certain costs as pipelines rupture and oil spews forth. Or we could analyze these environmental crises as inevitable outcomes of our effort to dominate nature in the interest of profit. The first frame would solve oil spills with better environmental protection measures and clean-ups, while the second frame would attempt to prevent them altogether, perhaps shifting away from the use of petroleum and natural gas and toward alternative energies that are "green."

These books introduce various frames such as these for viewing social problems. They also highlight debates between social scientists who frame problems differently. The books suggest solutions, both on the macro and micro levels. That is, they suggest what new policies might entail, and they also identify ways in which people, from the ground level, can work toward a better world, changing themselves and their lives and families and providing models of change for others.

Readers do not need an extensive background in academic sociology to benefit from these books. Each book is student-friendly in that we provide glossaries of terms for the uninitiated that are keyed to bolded terms in the text. Each chapter ends with questions for further thought and discussion. The level of each book is accessible to undergraduate students, even as these books offer sophisticated and innovative analyses.

People "overshare" when they interact with others through the screens of computers and smartphones. Oversharing means to divulge more of their inner feelings, opinions and sexuality than they would in person, or even over the phone. Text messaging, Facebooking, tweeting, camming, blogging, online dating, and Internet porn are vehicles of this oversharing, which blurs the boundary between public and private life. Ben Agger's book examines these "presentations of self," acknowledging that we are much more public about what used to be private. The book concludes with reflections on the impact of oversharing on identity, friendship, sexuality, family and democracy, and suggests steps people can take to re-establish the boundary between public and personal life.

Preface

For most of my life, I had to send a letter to make contact with another person, or call them from a telephone in my house or from a pay phone. I could visit them, knocking on the door. When I was in my 40s, all of this began to change. People could carry around their phones, many of which connected to the Internet, a strange new information and communication vehicle that did not make itself felt in my life until the 1990s. All of a sudden, people had the means to communicate globally, in nearly instantaneous ways. And they could use the Internet to sell things, shop, find dates and mates, even to watch **pornography**. This is a world I could not have imagined as a child growing up in the 1960s.

To be sure, we had television, while my father as a child only had radio. The assassination of President Kennedy in 1963, when I was 11, instantly made television a force to be reckoned with. We would now get much of our news and entertainment from that box in the living room. While we still read newspapers, an activity that the German philosopher Hegel called the prayer of the realist, our world was becoming electronic.

At first, the electronic media rendered us passive, and they still do in the case of television and movies (Adorno 1954; Miller 1988). Even here, more interaction is possible, as people can TiVo their shows and watch them later without advertising. But the Internet changed everything, allowing people to post their literary wares and send email. Eventually they could text and tweet. Readers became writers, making for a whole new involvement with electronic media. In particular, we can bare our soul for the public, or at least for our cellphone contacts and Facebook friends.

People "overshare" when they interact with others through the screens of computers and smartphones. Oversharing means to divulge more of their inner feelings, opinions and sexuality than they would in person, or even over the phone. Text messaging, Facebooking, tweeting, camming, blogging, online dating, and Internet porn are vehicles of this oversharing, which blurs the boundary between public and private life. Teenagers indicate their relationship status for all the world to see. Adults who date electronically construct themselves as hot, smart, in shape, affluent. And many men, and even some women, consume porn. Some even produce "amateur" porn depicting their own sexuality—the ultimate oversharing. This book examines these modes of the "presentation of self," acknowledging that we are much more public about what used to be private.

I am concerned about how oversharing reflects and reproduces certain personality disorders that hinder people's attempts to be happy. I am also concerned that oversharing in 160-character texts and even shorter tweets causes public discourse to decline. We have taken terrific literary vehicles—the Internet and now smartphones—and we use them for banal chatter, not for what really matters.

The book concludes with reflections on the impact of oversharing on identity, friendship, sexuality, family, and democracy. I seek ways to transform our pornographic public sphere, in which people bare their bodies and their innermost thoughts and desires. I suggest steps people can take in their own lives to avoid oversharing while also seeking intimacy, love, and community.

My account is sociological, even if few empirical studies have been conducted on these late-breaking developments in the lives of young people and their parents. I analyze our immersion in the swirl of immediacy—that which consumes us, and from which we have a hard time gaining distance. As Hegel (1967) wrote: "The True is the Bacchanalian revel in which no member is not drunk; yet because each member collapses as soon as he drops out, the revel is just as much transparent and simple repose." I love the young; I love my own children. I empathize with them as they suffer a world not of their making. We elders have burdened them with too much homework and too many adult expectations. It is no wonder they seek solace in their electronics. This book is self-criticism as well as social criticism. But I don't offer only a critique; I suggest utopia—different ways to live.

This book presents a framework for thinking about the dizzying cyberworld and its effects on the self and society. The conversation continues. There are no simple answers. I speculate. I talk to my students. I observe everyday behavior. It is difficult to have a firm grip. As Marx wrote, "all that is solid melts into air." Or, as one might add today, all that is solid dissolves into pixels.

1:   Thanks for Sharing

Erving Goffman suggested that we hold back our true selves when we interact, but, today, people disclose a lot more, perhaps because we hide behind our screen names.

Shakespeare gave the Canadian sociologist Erving Goffman one of the most powerful sociological concepts: All the world's a stage, and we are actors playing our parts. We are in effect reading from scripts, and frequently improvising when we forget our lines. This insight is developed in Goffman's (1959) book *The Presentation of Self in Everyday Life*, which remains one of the classic texts of **symbolic interactionism**.

Goffman used Shakespeare for his metaphor—the dramaturgical analogy. Imagine, he is saying, that we are playing the parts of Iago, Desdemona, Hippolyta, Hamlet. Before the play, we put on our costumes and makeup. If we are "method" actors, we inhabit the role so that it becomes "us," at least for the duration of the play. After the play is over, we slide out of costume, makeup and role, and return to our "real" selves and lives. We are backstage, where we can let our hair down and no longer play a theatrical role.

Goffman notices that, in our real lives, we are still playing roles. This is the great insight of sociology, which examines the social scripts that guide our behavior. But even here, there is a backstage—a place we could go and be ourselves. This place is the home, our anchor in private life. At least this is the way it used to be. I grew up straddling the 1950s and 1960s, when we began to shift the boundary between role playing and being real as electronic media came to dominate our culture and frame our experience. Now the world invades our living rooms and psyches; they are instantaneous, suggesting a verb "to instantaneize" that describes much of contemporary experience.

The Internet Blurs Boundaries

Everyone drinks deeply of the media, and with good reason. Or, at least, people do so who are connected electronically. Not everyone has a computer or smartphone. Some, especially baby boomers who knew typewriters and rotary phones, don't want them. Some cannot afford them. We learn, connect and are entertained in global, real-time ways. The media open the world to us, and allow us to write as well as read. We blog, email, text, tweet, not simply consuming information and insight, but producing them. However, the media penetrate the private world, what Goffman calls the backstage, in ways that change what it means to be a person, to have boundaries, to disclose our inner feelings. Rapid and global technologies of information, communication and entertainment cause us to **overshare**, the key issue addressed in this book. This is Emily Gould's (2008) term for revealing "too" much about ourselves. Of course, how much is too much depends on the context and the people involved!

Controversy swirls around Gould, who used to work for Gawker (gawker.com), a blog that posted gossip about celebrities and tracked their New York City whereabouts, based on citizen reports. Recently, she published a revealing memoir, *And the Heart Said Whatever*, chronicling her life so far (Gould 2010). The book described much about her dating, sex and work. She somewhat regrets her earlier oversharing in her blogging, but she does so in a book that could be considered an overshare. It is difficult not to wince at some of her confessions. In this age of information and instantaneity, it is perhaps not surprising that people overshare. The Internet and smartphones make information gathering, chatting and texting daily habits for billions of people. But these technologies are also invasive, intruding in our time and place. We are now available 24/7, and Internet addiction is a risk. (For a discussion of the sociology of cell or mobile phones, see McGuigan 2005 and Rippin 2005.)

And now there is the biggest vehicle of oversharing of all—Facebook! One posts all of one's personal details, relationship status, likes and dislikes, pictures and postings of friends, of whom one can have hundreds or even thousands. This is the personal made totally public, although one can restrict access to one's personal page. Now, one is exposed to the world, including friends of friends, and their friends. "To friend" has become a verb of the early 21st century. One invites a person to be one's friend, and they accept, reject, or just ignore—the cruelest fate of all. Not to be outdone, Google has launched a competitor, Google+.

Twitter is another engine of oversharing. This is not for deep reflections. As with texting, one is restricted to a few sentences' worth of characters, making for short postings indeed. One "tweets" about one's day, what one is doing and thinking, one's ephemeral opinions. One can do the same sort of hour-by-hour posting on Facebook. Begley (2011) talks of the "Twitterization" of our culture.

The vehicle of these electronic interventions is the computer. But the computer, no longer a clunky and massive mainframe, is now a laptop or even a telephone—a cellphone termed a smartphone, one with Internet connectivity and keyboarding capability. People connect every minute of their waking hours, checking their email, their Facebook page, text messages, tweets. They both read and write—the sound-byte messages littered with shorthand, code, and emoticons. LOL.

This book is about the various ways in which the private is becoming public, perhaps impoverishing the private self and littering the public sphere with the detritus of mere opinion and chatter. This is already elitist-sounding, with learned sages monopolizing the public sphere of ideas and opinion. I am in favor of democracy, but not necessarily of **deboundarying**, which is what is taking place today. I favor connection, but not necessarily round-the-clock connectivity. We gain the world but lose ourselves in it.

And yet. Who doesn't love the Internet, the phone, the laptop? Who doesn't love getting email and texts? In this book, I distinguish between narcissism (Lasch 1979) and a culture of dialogue, between oversharing and a talkative cyberdemocracy. The boundary between these two is flimsy and permeable, requiring judgment on the part of analysts and citizens.

Sharing used to mean splitting your dessert with your significant other. Now, it means spilling your guts, going public with intimate details of your life. Oversharing is telling too much. But how do we determine how much is too much? I will ask what is good for the person's mental health and also what is good for democracy. I will consider what is good for the family and relationships. All of these are considerations of boundaries, notably between what we should "share" and what we should conceal.

Concealment is not the same as deception. Sharing might involve deception, such as lying about your age. Concealment might mean not telling your date everything about your past on the first date, including your struggle with alcohol. One can conceal by failing to disclose. One can also conceal by lying and spinning, portraying oneself as svelte and youngish when, in fact, one is overweight and a senior citizen. I will visit these issues when I address Internet dating.

My account is necessarily about young people as well as their parental elders. Young people use digital technologies adeptly; they live their lives on the screen as well as face-to-face. The Digital Youth Research Project, linking scholars at University of Southern California and University of California at Berkeley, has pioneered research into young people's digital cultures. The late Peter Lyman, at Berkeley's School of Information, led this initiative. A list of publications and reports collected by scholars involved in this initiative, funded by the MacArthur Foundation, can be found at http://digitalyouth.ischool.berkeley.edu/publications. Studies on nearly all the topics I discuss in this book can be found at that website, an invaluable database and library on these late-breaking issues.

Too Much Information: Gossip, Drama, Spinning and Playing

Oversharing can be unpacked theoretically. There are two dominant features. People who overshare *immerse themselves in banality*, gossiping and trading factoids about their everyday lives and the everyday lives of others. Of course, this is not restricted to the Internet. *People* magazine is a site of this immersion. We inhabit a **gossip culture**. People who overshare also *seek connection and community*. They desire to find and cultivate friendships. Facebook even transforms this into a verb: **to friend**. People seek friends online because they don't have enough face-to-face friends. Or, as we learn, the boundary between Facebook friends and "real" friends is highly permeable, requiring us to be suspicious of a sharp distinction between the two.

Oversharing involves or leads to gossip, drama, spinning and playing. Oversharing, by definition, is "too much information" (**TMI**)—the posting or promulgating of highly personal information, such as one's relationship status. Sometimes, when faced with TMI in face-to-face conversation, the listener covers her ears and says "too much information," which means, "I don't want to hear about your sex life or how you cheated on an exam." I contend that TMI is partly a function of narcissism, wanting to shout out loud about one's uniqueness, and partly a result of the fact that people can, in effect, hide behind their computer screens and even their screen names. Of course, gossip and TMI are connected; the self-revelation of personal thoughts and actions provides fodder for gossip. Indeed, in a sense TMI and gossip could be identical when the person is promoting gossip about herself.

Gossip includes exchanging secrets and information about other people, whether celebrities or people in one's own everyday world. Gossip necessarily involves three or more parties. A tells B something about C, or perhaps A tells B that C said something about B. Gossip is often false or exaggerated; its credibility is not to be trusted, especially if it is found on the Internet, where the boundary between experts and amateurs blurs to the point of near-indistinguishability.

We are intensely interested in the banalities of everyday life because we all have everyday lives. We are somewhat voyeuristic and also somewhat exhibitionist; we love to learn salacious things about our fellows and we love to expose ourselves to them. This sounds like a sexual kink, but, in fact, it is a deep-seated part of our social nature—to see and to be seen in the ordinary lives we lead. In a sense, this is a reaction to what Guy Debord (1983) calls the society of the spectacle, the gargantuan productions of Hollywood and Madison Avenue that put distance between ourselves and the stars we idolize—Jennifer Aniston, George Clooney, LeBron James. These are people who have been heroized and inflated. We want to bring them back to earth and cut them down to size, learning about Jenn's divorce or LeBron's love–hate affair with the city of Cleveland.

And we want to connect with others because we are alone in the world, perhaps even lonely. Our kids are a lot less lonely than they would be without their smartphones, which allow them to text each other, forming a secret society of kids and adolescents. We want connection and we also seek community, which is connection multiplied by dozens, hundreds and thousands. When we connect, we trade intimacies, opinions, gossip. We especially chatter about what I am calling the banalities of everyday life— our own, yours, hers, his. This is the voyeuristic and exhibitionist side of our natures, the wanting to watch and be watched side. We are intrigued by the misfortunes that befall others; the German word for this is *Schadenfreude*, enjoying the misfortunes of others, especially the high and mighty. Of course, we, the gullible public, transform the Anistons and Clooneys into big stars, flocking to the box office to see their latest movie vehicles. And then we tear them down or at least drool when we watch them take a fall. Kim Kardashian is the lastest victim of her own fame.

But we don't only gossip about the rich and famous. We gossip about our neighbors, the girl in 11th grade chemistry, the couple from work who just hooked-up. A great deal of Internet chatter purveys this sort of gossip, which springs from curiosity about other people's everyday lives. We insert ourselves into these lives through social media such as Facebook—befriending, unfriending, posting. In so doing, our oversharing manufactures **drama**, which involves acting out and other types of emotional display.

Although no one will admit to liking drama, drama is intriguing, especially if it includes other people. Drama often involves the delivery of gossip: "He said he really likes you, but is still into his ex." And the gossip can deceive, especially if the production of drama is intended to serve one's own emotional purposes. "He said he is done with you and wants to move on" might well conceal a motive to date "him." Drama posted on Facebook, texted, or tweeted may also involve the observation of dubious behavior: "She was flirting at the bar." Drama is a category of gossip, and usually involves people in relationships, or seeking them. Drama is often intensified by oversharing, especially TMI.

Oversharing also involves **spinning**—air-brushing one's flaws, telling tall tales, outright lying. We see spinning on dating websites but also on Facebook as people construct themselves. The socially constructed nature of identity on the Internet is a crucial factor in understanding how we make the private public, in effect transforming ourselves into the selves we would like to be. I contend that there is a good deal of what Freud (1991) called wish fulfillment involved in all forms of oversharing, especially TMI and spinning; we become more interesting, intelligent, attractive. Spinning and playing, discussed immediately below, are not exactly TMI, but they involve *mis*information or even *dis*information. For example, I know a woman who claimed to know a lot about baseball. I asked her to explain the hit-and-run play, and she couldn't do it, even though she played intramural softball in college.

There is a curious reversal here: People overshare, but they partly conceal their "real" self, the actor, backstage and offstage, who takes off their makeup and puts on street clothes. They share their surface self, not the deeper, "real" one. The drama-loving, gossip-mongering person may be out of touch with who they really are. We call people, especially men, who are insincere in their romantic relationships "players," which involves spinning. What they are really playing are roles—various façades that they try on and take off for different others with whom they are involved. **Playing**, then, is calculated role playing wherein the self strategically seeks to be different things to different people. Playing may also involve sexuality, which, if inflected by TMI, takes the form of pornography, especially the amateur kind. After all, players play. Players also "play" other people (i.e. deceive others). Players are only called players because their play is obvious—they are not "smooth."

The Self Under Siege: The Psychiatry of Oversharing

This discussion requires us to think deeply about a key issue addressed by postmodernism. Is there a stable, solid core self or is the person, in effect, a "subject position," an oversharer who constructs herself to fit the situation—a vegetarian on Tuesday, a Republican on Wednesday, a swinger on Friday? Players tell you what you want to hear; they are involved in sales or marketing—here the marketing of the self. Must we behave this way, or is this avoidable? And is it a kind of emotional disorder, what psychiatrists term a personality disorder or mood disorder? The oversharing, drama-seeking, gossiping, playing self could be said to have serious emotional problems that involve the lack of a stable identity.

There are two personality disorders that seem to capture many elements of the oversharing self: **narcissistic personality disorder** (NPD) and **borderline personality disorder**. The true narcissist is given to grandiosity—an inflated sense of self but, underneath, low self-esteem. The borderline personality (borderline meaning just this side of psychosis) is given to impulsive risk-taking (e.g., sex without protection) and is clingy, but sometimes engages in "splitting," which means she swings from idealizing her partner to demonizing (hating) him. Both disorders flow from low self-esteem, which may stem from early-childhood or adolescent abuse or neglect. Descriptions of these disorders can be found in the *Diagnostic and Statistical Manual of Mental Disorders (DSM-IV-TR)*, published by the American Psychiatric Association (2000). Interestingly, the fifth edition of the DSM, due out in 2013, eliminates NPD from its list of personality disorders on the ground that its traits can be found in several personality disorders.

Sociologists since Durkheim (1950) are loath to speculate about what is going on in people's heads. They prefer to concentrate on observable, often measurable behavior. But I am interested in the mind–body connection, even if we must make certain inferences about what happens to people on the inside. I am interested in the psychiatry of oversharing, especially about narcissistic and borderline personality disorders. There is a risk in implying that psychological problems can be fixed or cured by medication. But there is a great deal of psychological and emotional unrest among our people, and we often, in our Puritanical but pornographic culture, ignore this, believing that only crazy people need help and that the rest of us mere neurotics can help ourselves! Instead, the psychologist and sociologist should be the closest of allies as many of our problems of living are problems on the inside, and between intimates.

I (Agger 2011a) have written about body problems of a fat- and sugar-larded diet, without adequate exercise. Here, I am writing about emotional problems sometimes termed personality disorders and mood disorders by psychiatrists. But I am viewing these problems as essentially social in nature, occurring between people, perhaps, as Freud speculated, stemming from our earliest relations with our parents. Body problems and emotional problems are connected, especially as we traffic in bodies when we sext, Internet date, and produce and consume pornography. Oversharing often has a distinctly sexual dimension.

Both narcissistic and borderline personality disorders involve low self-esteem and the lack of self-worth. It is easy for people in our pornographic, soul-baring culture to have low self-esteem. There are several reasons for this:

- We cannot measure up to cultural icons who seem to dwarf us and to be perfect.
- We spend much of our work and school lives in relationships of hierarchy and we are constantly berated and beaten down.
- Our parents may not have parented us sufficiently because they had their own demons and/or got divorced, breaking up the family.
- We may have been abused, sexually or emotionally, in our childhood, carrying forward the trauma.
- We may have weak ties with people who are connected to us electronically.

Narcissists exhibit a certain grandiosity, a sense of self-importance, even when they feel hollow inside. Much of this is posturing. Borderlines feel empty and may hop from bed to bed in search of connection, which they then shun. These are self-defeating paths, but they compel their victims; these are not rational choices.

The Internet is a breeding ground of grandiosity as people crow about themselves and express their opinions. It also breeds the search for intimacy, even if this is electronic and not face-to-face. Electronic intimacy can be turned on and off at will. Three-dimensional intimacy requires commitment and reciprocity.

It is difficult to read oversharing as anything but narcissism, a projection of the self onto others. Too, oversharing involves the instant intimacy of borderlines, who hook-up and glom on almost immediately, before they turn away. Internet oversharing does not cause these two personality disorders, but people predisposed to narcissistic and borderline syndromes are drawn to texting, Facebooking, pornography, and online dating hook-ups. Internet oversharing facilitates people already destined to have these personality disorders, thereby intensifying them.

I am not suggesting that American psychiatry includes oversharing as a mood disorder, although it includes troubling features such as a plastic sense of self, self-absorption, and being all things to all people. Oversharers have what some psychologists call **thin boundaries**, that is, they are easily influenced by other people. In fact, they are so immersed in banality, as I termed it above, that they lack core values and a stable identity and simply reflect popular culture, media, and gossip.

How many hours a day must one spend on Facebook, texting, dating online, or watching porn to be viewed as having an oversharing disorder? I wish I knew! It is not simply time spent on these oversharing pursuits but *the way in which the person loses herself in the world*, which is what happens to the oversharer. Thin boundaries refer to the boundary between the person and the world, the private and public selves. We need to be able to retreat into a solid, stable identity and values, albeit genuinely connected to other people. After all, the oversharing self is reaching out, clamoring for attention—for friends and for love, even if the friends are Facebook "friends," who are earned cheaply.

Technology plays a huge role in enabling the person to be lost in the world. Without text messaging and Facebook, let alone email, oversharing wouldn't go "viral" at the rate at which it now does. When I was a teenager in the 1960s, there were no technological means for oversharing, apart from the old-fashioned rotary telephone (of which many people had just one) and old-fashioned snail mail. One could always sneak a peek at his sister's diary, but writing in one's diary is hardly oversharing; it is intimate information intended to be kept private. And there was a gossip culture at school, but it was of the non-viral word-of-mouth kind, where Johnny told Mary who told Susie. While there could be gossip, drama, TMI, spinning, and playing, these were not conducted nearly at the speed of light but through the slow circuitries of pre-Internet America. And our only pornography was *Playboy*, which is tame compared to Internet porn sites.

Gloria Jacobs (2009, 2008, 2006) has done important work on adolescent identity, attention seeking, and Internet interaction and writing. She notices that kids write furiously, both to enrich their identities and to form community, even if many of these non-traditional formats such as instant messaging and texting fall below the adult radar screen. We need to learn to read our kids, even if what they write is encoded in emoticons and hasty texts instead of term papers on Mark Twain or the origin of slavery. Of course, the two types of literacy can enrich each other, as Jacobs knows.

And so there has been interaction between the technologies of sharing, such as the Internet and texting, and cultural and emotional changes that cause the self to be immersed in everyday life, even losing herself there. People inhabit a gossip culture from which they also seek connection and community. They now possess the means of connection, but their sharing involves TMI and may lead to drama—not more substantive issues such as politics and personal philosophies. This is not to suggest that these rapid and global technologies can't be used for more elevating purposes; I am composing this book on a laptop, from which I also periodically check my email.

Which is chicken and egg—a gossip culture or narcissism? They are two sides of the same coin, which is the immersion of the self in everyday life, as opposed to gaining healthy distance from it. Narcissistic gossipers and posters are not intellectuals, that is, people who methodically distance themselves from the mere appearances of reality. Intellectuals dig underneath the surface; they ask what things really mean. They don't take the world's word for it—advertising slogans, Facebook or dating-site profiles, emoticon-riddled text messages composed and sent quickly. Time is a major component of this discussion, which is really a discussion of human identity within a **fast capitalism**. I characterize the compressed, elastic time of people who are constantly plugged in as **iTime** (Agger 2011b).

It is simply easier, more convenient, less of a hassle to compose a brief text message, email, or Facebook post than to ponder the complexities of the war in Afghanistan, global warming, the role of China in the world economy, the nature of justice. I have yet to weigh the evidence fully about whether people are by nature lazy or energetic, and I am in my late 50s! Some social scientists would like to believe that we are nothing "by nature," that everything we are is simply imprinted on us through social experience. But we have bodies and we inherit certain DNA configurations from our parents. The boundary between human nature and society is certainly complex and worth thinking about. I am fairly certain that we all need love and nurturance, and, similarly, we need to be challenged creatively by work and leisure that we enjoy (Maslow 1970).

And so perhaps we are by nature people who crave calorie-dense food like chocolate and who compose short messages immersed in the gossip of the moment. Perhaps it is much more difficult to eat our broccoli and think reflectively about the human condition. But let's also give social science its due: Regardless of what or who we are by nature, we are taught to be stupid, lazy, uninquisitive. Our culture tempts us to gossip, just as we are tempted to eat processed foods full of salt and high-fructose corn syrup.

And that raises what is perhaps my most important issue. How are we—people of a literary and sociable and even political nature—to share without oversharing, to respect the boundary between private and public while trying, with energy and elan, to change the public world? Where does useful information leave off and TMI begin? When does the world not need to know what I had for dinner last night, or my relationship status, or where I attended high school?

By my sixth and concluding chapter, on a healthy **public sphere** in which pornography is not the standard of self-revelation, I approach a practical answer to those questions of how much information is too much. My discussion of pornography, in my fifth chapter, will point the way toward an answer. We all know pornography when we see it; we don't need so-called community standards to tell us. I want to live in a society in which the public sphere, another word for cyberspace and old-fashioned urban space, too, is not pornographic, even though I hasten to add that I am not opposed to pornography. I don't think it causes violence against women, and nor do I think it rots the souls of the young. Pornography overshares, and transforms sexuality into a spectator sport. It removes the boundaries around a wonderful private act, as I will argue in the pornography chapter later. I explore the ways in which we can keep private life private while enhancing a public sphere based on sharing, empathy, community. Without maintaining a boundary between private and public, we lose ourselves to a public world that is primarily pornographic, that is, in which private acts become public images.

DISCUSSION QUESTIONS

1. How do you deal with the fact that there is a lot of information out there and that it is easy to be distracted?
2. Why is gossip so intriguing? Do you gossip and, if so, do you feel guilty about doing so?
3. Is it easier for you to overshare in writing or face-to-face? Why is this?

II: Texting, Tweeting, and Blogging

Young people may not turn in their term papers on time, but they write furiously in non-traditional forms, telling their many stories.

Just a few years ago, no one had ever heard of texting and tweeting. There were no text messages and no Twitter. People had begun to post blogs, but blogging had not yet become a widely-understood verb. To blog or not to blog, that is the question. Now, everyone, it seems, texts and many tweet and some blog. The young, especially, text. To text: to write and send brief electronic messages using one's phone.

It takes me forever to compose a text, even if I use a word-recognition function that allows the phone to guess that I am writing "house" or "surrogate." This activity of composition is like hunting and pecking on an old-fashioned typewriter; I can't touch type the way some people can on their smartphones. My fingers feel too big for the keys.

I'm old, and old school. Phones are for placing calls, not texting, surfing the Web, or listening to music. I like land-lines, not mobile phones. To be sure, I lug around my laptop, doing my writing and checking my work email. I even took out a Facebook account in order to see what I was missing. I since resigned, having the uncomfortable feeling that I was watching my "friends" naked! And I once read the tweets of Andy Roddick, an American tennis star, in order to share his workout regimen with my teenage son, a budding tennis player in his own right.

I text my kids; they know no other way to connect with me. I try to impose a two-text rule, after which we make old-fashioned phone calls! But rarely do my kids or other kids call; they hide behind the miniature screen and type out their missives, perhaps avoiding intimacy and controlling the conversation. As well, texting can be hidden from adults, especially during the school day.

Positioning the Self, Leaving a Trail

Texting and tweeting position the self. These locate the person in a public world. Some phones have apps that allow precise GPS positioning. But I am talking about locating the user, especially the adolescent, in time and place. My college students check their phones when they leave class, retrieving and sending messages. They do the same thing in class when they think I'm not looking! They may text, Facebook, or tweet, keeping in touch with the world, even if they don't have substantive conversations. What counts as "substantive" is a key issue in this book. I am not dismissing chitchat, which can have a friendly tone. But the writing being conducted is not the reasoned, complex or lengthy composition involved in writing an essay or recording one's thoughts in a diary. Blogging is more like journaling and keeping a diary, requiring one to step back from everyday life in order to appraise it. People who blog are writers, as are all of us who express ourselves.

This self-positioning is like leaving a trail, an electronic one. Kids may feel isolated, without a tight community, friends, or lovers. They work hard to establish connections, and texting is perfect for this. Texts require little work to write or read, and reciprocity is easy, barely diverting people from their tasks at hand, sometimes including driving. And so there is a link between self-positioning and leaving a trail for others, especially loved ones. The texter is crying out "Here I am; notice me!" Unanswered texts leave one hanging, and the etiquette about when to close down the conversation is delicate. It would be less delicate if one were talking on the phone, but then more would be risked emotionally. Texting has no tone of voice or inflection; and it is byte-like, without the need to write more than a few sentences. Alford (2011) discusses email etiquette in much the same vein as he explores why people don't always embrace norms of timely reciprocity.

This enforced brevity is interesting. It requires a certain linearity of thought and expression. It is easy to see how texting would facilitate making arrangements for seeing a movie—which one, when, where—but young people and even their elders use the byte-like framework for working out more complicated issues, which require an exhaustive and exhausting back-and-forth. Texting is perfect for oversharing because the typed/texted word allows one to believe that she is venturing less emotionally because one can't hear the tone or undertone of the human voice. "I want to have sex with you" sounds entirely different when uttered than when typed. It is far less embarrassing to say and to hear when this is typed/texted than when uttered, although the character limit allows for less nuance when texting. "Sex" stands in for "making love," although one could abbreviate "love" into "luv."

Texting, unlike talking on the phone or face-to-face, is asynchronous; it can be conducted in a discontinuous way, with messages not requiring immediate responses. The receiver has a chance to compose herself, literally and figuratively, when she receives the text described in the preceding paragraph. Although one can look away from phone calls and listen to them on voice mail, returning the call risks a live conversation and loss of control over the dialogue. Texting, like emailing, gives one control over dialogue and hence reduces the risks involved in spontaneity.

Why, then, do people who text in order to conceal themselves also reveal themselves by texting, tweeting and blogging? They position themselves and leave a trail because they crave connection, but they are fragile and don't want to venture too much in spontaneous dialogue. It is curious that this would lead to oversharing, but my thesis is that people reveal more when they don't confront the voice and face of the other. It is easier to break up with someone in writing than in person, even if this is a serious breach of the social contract. Borderline personalities cannot face the truth in person because they fear rejection. They crave connection and thus they approach, but they then avoid; they attach but don't commit. They love and then hate, moving effortlessly from idealization to demonization, one of the hallmarks of borderline personality disorder. Oversharing in writing is a way of obtaining intimacy, even though conducting a relationship in writing is ultimately unfulfilling because it deprives the parties to it of the touch and voice.

Today, our relationships are mediated by the screen, behind which we hide our feelings and our vulnerability. This redoubles our vulnerability because it deprives us of face-to-face intimacy. This is not necessarily an either/or: Lovers can text and tweet in the interest of efficiency. However, one imagines that they spend most of their relationship in person and in voice. There is approach and avoidance in texting and tweeting: We want others to know where we are but not who we are. This would not seem to be oversharing, except that there is a sheer volume of contacts. Teenagers can send thousands of texts a month, and intimate information is bound to seep through. This is oversharing by comparison to the sharing of yesteryear, when I was a kid and young adult. I couldn't possibly have signaled my whereabouts and feelings to my significant others, except by telephone, when I and they were similarly grounded in space and time.

My son's friends will sometimes text me when they can't keep track of him. Oversharing here takes the form of instant accountability, which is a kind of oversharing. I resent it when my archaic but still textable cellphone vibrates with a new text and I am driving or doing something that I deem important! On the other hand, I recognize how this can become an addiction—this self-positioning and leaving a trail. We all crave connection, especially where we lack it in so many compartments of our lives. Texting is a substitute form of community. Indeed, for people who also enjoy face-to-face community, texting *is* community, a way for people who care about each other to stay in touch.

It is tempting for we elders, brought up in a pre-Internet era, to disdain electronic connection as inferior to the "real" thing—voice to voice, body to body. But I am noticing that these are two sides of the same coin; both are ways to stay connected. We leave a trail until we meet. Only when what I am calling leaving a trail through a purely electronic connection replaces face-to-face contact do we have a problem. The problem is inauthenticity—the way in which there are limits to human satisfaction when interaction is conducted completely in writing.

People are actually more reluctant to overshare in person than in writing. Looking into someone's eyes places constraints on how much one will disclose, such as "I love you" or "I want to have sex with you." The fear of rejection is greater in person than in writing, and so people venture more when they text, tweet, and email, or when they contact each other on dating sites. But venturing more is not necessarily a good thing for two reasons: People, when writing and posting, lie and spin, a tendency that is constrained by examining body language and the look in people's eyes; and people may say things they don't really intend or intend to do, taking interpersonal risks that would seem rash in face-to-face interaction.

To be sure, electronic connections may not involve oversharing for very shy people, which could include all teenagers on the planet! Here, Facebook and texting are made to order, as they allow kids the opportunity to disclose themselves to their intimates. But on Facebook, this disclosure is adult-like, such as when kids indicate their relationship status. Every adult knows that teenagers shouldn't be in "relationships." It is fine for them to date casually, but being "in a relationship" can be tantamount to being married, perhaps explaining why teenagers stay coupled today longer than we did in high school, back in the distant past of the 1960s. There is pressure, both from within and from others, to stay "in a relationship" when, in fact, they would rather be single and exploring. Every teenager who Facebooks knows how rapidly people's relationship status can change, and everyone knows someone who was dumped on Facebook, perhaps noticing that the person they thought was their girlfriend has suddenly become "single" again, according to her Facebook status.

I have much to say later on about Facebook. It is a significant site of oversharing today. But so are Internet dating services, also discussed later. And so is texting, which encourages disembodied communication, at lower risk than face-to-face communication, nearly every waking hour of the day. Texting is a communication machine, a way of positioning and leaving a trail that, in its sheer volume of interactions, produces an orgy of sharing. Whether this is oversharing depends in part on the extent to which people are merely exchanging information, such as when the next showing of the movie will start, or whether they are baring their souls, activities better left to face-to-face interaction, where there will be blushing and averted eyes but perhaps also hugging.

Prison Code and Vampirization

Every teenager knows someone, probably themselves, who defied authority and texted while at school! Hoodies are perfect for hiding phones. One can delete texts and keep them hidden from parents. And kids' texts are often written in codes, with acronyms and emoticons perhaps unfamiliar to adult readers. I view this as **prison code**, the protest of inmates against adult authority and a vehicle for building counter-community. Kids use texting, particularly at night, to stay off the adult radar screen, allowing them to tap on the walls of their cells in making connections.

As a kid, I had to use a public telephone in my house if I wanted to talk to my fellows. We could hang out after school, and we did, away from the prying eyes of parents. But as all-American boys, we spent our time playing sports, not gossiping. Texting is an activity unto itself, a literary activity. Kids don't play outside after school, for the most part, both because neighborhoods aren't public spaces in the way they used to be and because their time is taken up with mountains of homework and other resume-building activities.

And so kids claim the late night and very early morning as their adult-free zone. They text and Facebook, maintaining connection even though they are physically separated, as prisoners are. They joke, complain, flirt, build solidarity. They talk the talk of badasses, and they live as vampires (Goodale 2010), coming out only under cover of darkness. Parents don't supervise this activity, except perhaps to tell them that phone contact must cease by a certain time. Kids also use their laptops to Facebook and email, sometimes simultaneously using their phone to text and laptop to game or play music. These multimedia kids can multi-task, and they can have multiple conversations at the same time.

This is their leisure time, after homework, dinner, and activities have ended. They sleep less than we did, often having to arise only five or six hours after they finally go to sleep. Chronic sleep deprivation haunts the young, and also their sleep-deprived parents, who may be connected, too, watching television, surfing the Internet, viewing porn. (For a discussion of sleep in children's lives, see Lowe et al. 2007.) The image of a family sitting around the dinner table manipulating their smartphones is a contemporary version of the image, from my era, of families using TV trays to eat while watching television. We are good at being alone together (Turkle 2011).

Kids vamp and text because they can—they possess the technological means, which fits in their pocket or purse. And they do this because nighttime is their only time away from adult supervision. Many parents give up the idea of a curfew because, frankly, these are self-entertaining mechanisms, much as television used to be a baby-sitter. Kids still watch television, but they often text while they do. And texting takes time spent in composing messages and awaiting responses, which, because brief, will prompt a cycle of messages, perhaps lasting hours until bedtime. They possess the technology for nighttime contact, and they quickly discover that the technology possesses them. Even adults have trouble negotiating who should send the "last" text.

Adults allow their kids to inhabit a secret world because they pass them off to their technological baby-sitters and because they abbreviate their kids' childhoods, expecting them to behave like adults. We pile on the homework and other extracurriculars, especially now that we seek to emulate the Asian model of parenting ("tiger mothers" [Chua 2011]) glorified in a recent book. And then we are in bed by the time our kids are done with their exhausting days, which are far longer than the 9-to-5 days worked by many adults. We may even allow our kids to have alcohol, rationalizing that it is better that they drink at home than on their own. We want our kids to like us, thus becoming "cool" parents. And some parents have their own relationship issues to deal with; they in effect become the children as they pursue their post-divorce dating lives.

There is a flexible boundary between kids' and adults' texting. Like their kids, adults, too, text, tweet, email, and blog. They even use Facebook and other social media. We are all plugged in, creating community where none may have existed before. We all hide behind our screens, and we compose ourselves on the screen, often in ways that do not exactly mimic reality (see Turkle 1995). Yes, the digital divide contains a generational divide, with kids ahead of the curve when it comes to phone and Internet use. But adults are catching up, sometimes with their kids' help.

Yet adults are dominant, setting the educational and family agendas. To be sure, we all need teachers and parents. Yet, as we (Agger and Shelton 2007) contend, children and teenagers are a forgotten and neglected minority group, powerless and put upon by adults who resent the freedom their kids enjoy. And so we pile on the work and ratchet up the expectations, even idealizing the tiger-mother author, who wants her kids not to have fun, experiment, explore, socialize—all in the name of getting into Harvard. There is something profoundly abusive about telling your kids that they have to be first in their classes, or else; that they have to have all As, or else. This is child abuse by any name. It can be defended as the means to an end: Ivy-League education. But very few American teenagers end up at Harvard, Yale, Brown or Princeton. Half of them don't go to college at all, and many attend community colleges and four-year institutions.

Stress is the 21st century manifestation of **alienation**, Marx's 19th century term for having lost control of one's life and feeling hopeless. People de-stress by using drugs and alcohol, exercising, sharing their issues with others. The early sociologist Emile Durkheim (1951) noticed that people with abundant social ties are less likely to commit suicide than those who don't. He found that Catholics are less suicide-prone than Protestants because they are enmeshed in the fabric of the local church and can use the priest as, in effect, a social worker or psychiatrist, whereas Protestants seek a direct relationship with a silent god. Prison talk is a way of making time pass more quickly, of sharing the pain of incarceration. Imprisonment is an extreme predicament, and no one believes that prison rehabilitates. Childhood is a kind of prison in which adults are the enemy, constantly judging youngsters and imposing work and rules on them. No wonder that young people turn into texting vampires, as do some of their parents, who increasingly are inseparable from their phones in order to stay in touch.

The analogy of texting to prison communication between inmates breaks down where the inmates are actually planning a jail break. Today, **jailbreaking** among young people means to "free" the phone from a contractual relationship or limitation, to liberate, for example, your iPhone from AT&T so it can be used on another carrier. **Cracking** allows an app to run on a phone for free. To be sure, people can use texting in order to plan for a movie. But for the most part, texts are unmemorable; they are chatter, throw-away messages that merely divert and entertain. They can't be deep philosophy because they are limited in length. And they tend to be composed hastily, the type of signaling I described in the last section. At night, especially, texting may involve letting off steam or, as I discuss in the following section, expressing a certain sexual desire.

Sexting

"Text" used to be only a noun, referring to a written work. Today text is a verb that transposes into a different verb, when blended with the noun "sex." **Sexting** involves sending sexual messages or pornographic photos and videos. Of course, laptops already make this possible, via email and webcams. Texts differ from emails only in that one sends them to a phone number, not an email address, which frequently ends with the suffix .com or .edu. One can write a sexy email and attach an explicit photo, just as one can use instant messaging or the mail function of a dating website to do the same things.

Sexting is controversial because young people, who text frenetically, use their phones as vehicles for sex talk and sexual images. This should not be a surprise inasmuch as teenagers think about sex a lot! But adults who view sexuality as sinful have almost no control over their kids' "sexting" and kids use texting as a vehicle not only of complaints about adults—prison code—but as a medium of sexual self-expression. Not all young people sext; C.J. Pascoe, a sociologist at Colorado College, surveyed young people and found that few send sexy texts or photos (UPI 2009).

To be a celebrity today is risky because one's public behavior is now fair game for camera-wielding private citizens who post photos and videos on YouTube or perhaps offer them to sites such as TMZ. A phone is not only a phone and a computer but also a camera, transforming the boundary between public and private behavior without having the consent of the photographic subjects. This topic will emerge again in my discussion of pornography as I explore the distinction between what I term a **pornographic public sphere** and a **non-pornographic public sphere**.

In a pornographic public sphere, we find many visual images and videos of sexuality and we find ample public talk about sex. This public sphere is heavily voyeuristic and exhibitionist. People sext, webcam, and watch and make porn. In the pornographic public sphere, people explore kinkiness, a deviation from mainstream sexual practices and an exploration of tabooed sexuality, which is viewed as enticing. In a non-pornographic public sphere, sexual repression has been eased, there are few taboos, especially imposed by religion, and thus people are not as tempted to taste the forbidden fruit of kinky practices. There is less visualization and representation of sexuality, but more sexuality reframed as intimacy.

Sexting is the first example in this book of a pornographic public sphere. It is common for people, especially young people, to photograph themselves having sex, or their partner naked, and then to circulate these images virally using phones or laptops. This is not to suggest that sexting is "bad" or "wrong." People who inhabit a non-pornographic public sphere and who love each other can talk among themselves, using text messaging, about sexual intimacy. The very concept of kinky behavior only arises in a culture in which various sexual practices are taboo and thus tempt. Once these activities lose their **stigmas**, they become less enticing, which is a hallmark of a non-pornographic but sexually permissive public sphere.

Oversharing about sex occurs in a culture fascinated with tabooed sexual practices: **bondage**, **domination/submission**, **swinging**. The young are always fascinated by sex, but now, with the Internet, sexuality beckons at every turn. Sexting blends adolescent sexual energy with a pornographic culture in which sexual talk and imagery are abundant. Young people can produce their own porn using their phones, taking photos, camming, and producing sexual commentary. And this is conducted well below the adult radar screen, using phones that can be secreted away. Of course, as with the Internet, sexts can be circulated infinitely, moving one-on-one sexual discourse and imagery into the realm of public pornography, usually to the detriment of at least one partner's reputation.

Sexy texts and images sent using multimedia messaging services (MMS) blur the boundary between text and image, which is crucial for pornographic representation. Skype enables video calling, which takes phone sex to a new level, producing the same effect as webcams—sex performed and viewed in real time. Skype is interactive, enabling both parties to watch and be watched as they instant message each other.

One might question why our pornographic culture is so voyeuristic and exhibitionist. Understanding that will provide clues as to why people overshare. They are screaming "Look at me!" They may feel that no one is looking or caring. Combine this feeling of disconnection (Durkheim called it **anomie**) with tabooed sexuality and it is little wonder that people would share and overshare about their sexual desires and images. I am in favor of connection and removing taboos on sexual behavior between consenting adults, creating the non-pornographic public sphere I defined and defended above. Here, I am simply wondering what compels young and old to sext, consume Internet porn, and exhibit themselves having sex on their cams. They are deprived of something: love, meaning, identity, self-esteem, community, and connection. They are also obsessed with sex because many of us have been taught that sex is dirty and evil, making it that much more enticing.

The website Chatroulette (chatroulette.com) is the latest vehicle of this pornographic culture, a type of social media that connects people randomly via webcam. Developed by a teenager in Russia, this site allows people to accept or reject the opportunity to chat with total strangers, of whom the majority are probably in their early 20s or even younger. Perhaps this is a kind of undersharing, where rapid and random exposure via webcam leads nowhere, without substantive interactions. Perhaps oversharing automatically undershares in the sense that we don't learn what is really important about a person but merely exchange ephemeral gossip and trivia.

DISCUSSION QUESTIONS

1. Texting is efficient. But when does texting become a burden, an obligation?
2. On balance, is it good that kids have their own wired world, unavailable to adults?
3. Why do adults get so perturbed that kids use their phones for sexting? Is sexting unhealthy?

III: Social Media

Are a thousand Facebook friends worth two or three real friends?

The recent revolution in Egypt proceeded using Facebook. President Obama was elected and raised money using Facebook. The movie *Social Network*, depicting the roots of Facebook at Harvard in the imagination and hacking of Mark Zuckerberg, a mere undergraduate student, was a runaway hit. Everybody, it seems, is using Facebook (or FB) to "friend" each other, posting everyday trivia on their "walls" for all the world to view. Well, actually not all the world but only their "friends," of which one of my former friends has over 1,000! I had 43 FB friends, having been dragged into this folly by some of my students who want me to be cool and connected! I soldiered along, giving it a good-faith try. In fact, I could barely muster the energy to open up my Facebook page, which never seemed to contain much more than the following sequence of postings:

> "I had enchiladas for dinner."
> COMMENT: "You go, girl!"
> COMMENT: "Yum."

The fact that many people below the ages of 40 or 50 in industrial societies use Facebook makes it a worthy topic of sociological investigation. It is a fad and a trend. That many of the postings are no more than a single incomplete sentence is somewhat beside the point. More interesting is that "friends" friend each other—sending requests to be "friends" that are either accepted or ignored. One can view all the friends of one's friends, multiplying greatly the impact one can have through one's own postings. For a sustained reflection on leaving Facebook, see Hill (2009), who shares many of my criticisms. Brashears (forthcoming) discovers that people claim two close friends, whereas the average Facebook user boasts 130 "friends."

Facebook as the New Television (But Different)

As soon as I registered on Facebook, I noticed that some people were logged on all the time, day and night. And these are not only young people but also professionals

and professors. FB has become the new television, a mode of round-the-clock entertainment that, unlike TV, includes the possibility of interaction. Unlike television,
the person can be online surreptitiously while at work or via one's smartphone, thus
blurring the public/private and work/family boundaries.

I came to Facebook (and left) recently. I know that my kids are users, and most of
their friends. I know that most of my students are users. Recent data suggest that the
vast majority of Americans between 18 and 29 Facebook (a new verb of the times),
while just over half of older people use FB. These are staggering numbers, up from a
couple of years ago, when the Facebook trend was just getting underway. Before Facebook, there was MySpace, and other social-media sites are growing in number such as
Google+. But Facebook is the global gold standard for social media.

I compare FB to television because both can be entertaining and they can be left on
without requiring close attention. To be sure, television can be educational and require
focused attention, and FB can be used productively for work purposes. But both are
to be viewed on the screen and both occupy the whole viewing day and night. There
is no longer a test-pattern on television, signaling the demarcation between the end of
the viewing day and a restful night of sleep. These media are "on" 24/7, answering to
our round-the-clock need for diversion.

There is another reason for my comparison of TV and FB. They are not for the most
part "deep," requiring the serious application of intellect and critical analysis. Think
of the soap opera or the endlessly repeated segments of ESPN. Think of so-called reality television. Now, think of the FB "wall," with its self-revealing postings and the
string of "likes" and "comments" underneath them. My enchilada example, above, is
not a caricature; people post about the sheer minutiae of their days: I had a bottle of
wine with my spouse; we are waiting for our flight to take off; I am reading a certain
book or just saw a particular movie. These aren't weighty matters, but, then again,
must every moment of leisure time be devoted to reading and critically analyzing a
Dostoevsky novel?!

Televised situation comedies entertain because they remind us of ourselves, except
that they exaggerate our worst and best traits. The show *Modern Family* has something
for everyone: a gay couple with an adoptive infant from Asia; a sexy Latina; an Anglo
family with a neurotic but attractive mother and a realtor husband with a feminine
side; kids galore, of various levels of intellectual talent. Boundaries are blurred everywhere, between families, work and personal life, generations. They could be us, except
they are funnier and more attractive.

Facebook entertains us because it *is* us—our minute descriptions of our days, our
sensibility, our opinions. FB appeals to the exhibitionist and the voyeur. We can watch
the online versions of sit-coms, but in tiny bits and bytes. Worrell (2011) refers to this
as a process of granularization that also occurs when, for example, people transport a
tweet to FB. For those of us who are attentionally challenged, FB is the perfect vehicle:
Everyone can keep up. And, unlike television, we can intervene in the plot, altering it

ever so slightly with our own observations. And we can have a large cast, in the many hundreds and even thousands—our "friends" who have friends, who have friends. The network is potentially very vast and we can stay entertained by examining the lives of distant others.

FB is an anthropological vehicle, a way of studying the natives. We can see what the morning looks like for the girl with whom we went to high school, a work colleague abroad, our own kids and their friends. "I like your hair." "It is below zero here in the Midwest." These are the sound bytes of Facebook. And we can draw attention to our favorite music, food, literature, both displaying and adding to our cultural capital, as Bourdieu (1986) called it. One way to think about the strangeness of these practices is to imagine how an anthropologist from Mars would view them, a literary vehicle I use throughout this book! Thompson (2008) issues a topographical map of what he calls "the brave new world of digital intimacy."

These are not inherently interesting events. Like tweeting, these position us and help us leave a trail. In the case of FB, the trail is the series of postings, likes and comments that clutter the busy computer screen. But they are everyday events, **quotidian events**, that interest us because they are so banal. Our friends are people like us, much as the characters on *Modern Family* are like us in their eccentricity and expressiveness, even if they are somewhat prettier and funnier. The quotidian is comforting because it does not ask of us heroic effort. It is comforting because it is familiar. It is comforting because we can join the conversation, unlike television, where we must sit there passively.

I Like it: The Decline of Discourse

FB is comfort food for the contemporary soul. And yet I am not certain that this is good for civilization as we know it. The superficiality of FB postings entice us with their familiarity and unchallenging content, but they also cause **public discourse** to decline. One of my students noted that she receives likes and comments on her postings only when the postings are very brief. Paragraph-like constructions get ignored. I have had the same experience, although I never posted short, in sound bytes. I am too much the academic, the analyst, the scholar of Theodor Adorno (who wrote loooong sentences). Habits die hard. And clicking on the "like" icon conveys no meaning, at least to me. Do I like the person doing the posting? The posting? It is unclear. I rarely "comment" because I find that comments almost never lead to dialogue, building on each other.

The great thing about the Internet is that everyone can join the conversation if they have access. The troubling thing about the Internet is that everyone can join the conversation! **Cyberdemocracy** is the upside; the **decline of discourse** (Agger 1990) is the downside. The Internet is awash with mere opinion and crackpotism. Everyone has a theory about everything—the assassination of JFK, the first moon landing, the war in Iraq, whether life began with God's design or by sheer accident and then evolution. But some views are more studied and methodical, more academic and analytical, than others. I tell my students that they can begin their term papers by consulting Wikipedia, but only if they focus on the bibliography at the end, which contains real academic sources, both books and articles on the subject. Some Wiki entries are worthwhile and could pass for a scholarly encyclopedia. Other entries are sloppy and misleading.

I am not advocating that we police and patrol the Internet. The English philosopher John Stuart Mill (2003) talked in 1859 about a **marketplace of ideas**, a scholarly community, in which the strongest and best ideas would prevail over less-sound ideas. In the longer run, we can be confident that crackpot knowledge will fall by the wayside, trumped by sound scholarly knowledge. But in the meantime, the college student doing a term paper on President Kennedy's 1963 assassination Googles the topic and comes up with 726,000 results. How is she to judge the worthiness of this mind-boggling number of websites, especially if she judges (or is told) that Wikipedia is an inadequate source by itself?

Our First Amendment guarantees everyone the right to speak and publish freely. But does everyone have a right to an opinion? It was reported by MSNBC, the cable television network, that 51 percent of voters in the Republican Presidential primary in 2008 believed that President Obama was born outside of the United States, in Kenya presumably. This is staggering misinformation probably stemming from some voters' deep concerns about his race and religion. We suffer from what Russell Jacoby (1976) termed a **falling rate of intelligence**.

As well, our level of civic discourse could be higher than reality television shows such as *The Bachelor*, *Survivor*, and *American Idol*. Throw in Wikipedia, Facebook, and talk radio, and it is little wonder that our nation increasingly lags behind the levels of academic achievement and cultural literacy of European and Asian countries. We have experienced a decline of discourse that parallels the falling rate of intelligence. We produce and consume knowledge in bits and bytes, and mere opinion substitutes for real knowledge. It is good that everyone wants to be part of the conversation, but they need to be studious and analytical and the conversation, as I am calling it, needs to be about important matters. In a non-pornographic public sphere, people wouldn't simply lay themselves bare as they satisfy their voyeuristic and exhibitionist tendencies but they would read, study, and debate deep issues such as world overpopulation, global warming, domestic poverty, and the loss of neighborhood, among many other topics.

As print journalism migrates to the Internet, we forget the delight of savoring a thick newspaper that requires time and some elbow grease, as we leaf through the many pages, perhaps smearing ink on our fingers. The *Huffington Post* features some terrific journalism, but, for me at least, it is much less satisfying than sitting on the couch with my coffee devouring the *New York Times*. Newspapers are declining partly because they are losing precious revenue to Craigslist, which has nearly obliterated the classified advertising sections of newspapers. Craigslist is fine for consumers seeking used exercise equipment and perhaps even kinky sex. But the price we pay is the decline of journalistic discourse as people turn to the Internet for their news, and not necessarily to excellent sites such as *Huff Post* (www.huffingtonpost.com) but to the sound-byte journalism featured on Yahoo. Deep news analysis succumbs to headlines and capsule summaries, exactly what happens as Wikipedia replaces serious scholarship.

Is this a defense of books, newspapers, and libraries? It certainly is. I'd much rather hold a published book in my hands than a Kindle, which lacks the weight and gravitas of pulp. Yet I value not just the tactile qualities of books and newspapers; I am concerned about **discourse**, the ways in which we write and talk. Discourse has declined as mass popular culture, based on radio, television, movies, and now the Internet, has replaced an intellectual culture in which people consider ideas seriously.

It is easy to mistake the abundance of **information** for real **knowledge**. To be sure, if one has a cold, one can find thousands of pieces of advice. Some of these may be contradictory: Don't exercise with a cold, exercise with a cold. Take mega-doses of vitamin C; just drink some orange juice. If one is worried about having acquired HIV, a life-and-death matter, one can find very different advice about when to get an HIV test. These are tests that detect the antibodies the body produces to fight off the virus. Some websites indicate that the **window period** during which these antibodies begin to be produced is fully three months; that is what the Centers for Disease Control (CDC) in Atlanta suggests, making antibody tests (called ELISA) before three months worthless. Other sites state that antibodies can be detected after only six to eight weeks, given the sensitivity of recent fourth-generation antibody tests. This matters hugely because the sooner one begins to treat HIV, the longer is a person's life expectancy. Now, it is thought that people can live upward of 20 years or more with HIV if one starts a rigorous antiretroviral drug regime soon after diagnosis and then adheres to a regular drug protocol for life.

There are many excellent websites on HIV/AIDS, especially those developed by the CDC in Atlanta and university medical schools. Thebody.com offers excellent information. But there are other sites purporting that HIV is a myth, that it doesn't really exist. This is called **HIV denialism** (Smith and Novella 2007). By now, there isn't a respectable HIV researcher who doesn't believe that HIV/AIDS have laid waste to millions of lives. But if one consulted only the denialist websites, one would have a very different impression, and perhaps even refuse treatment.

Just as information and knowledge are different, so opinion and information are not necessarily the same. This is a hierarchy: everyone has opinions; certain opinions become information; and knowledge is information that is bona fide, having been rigorously researched.

Unfortunately, given the ease with which people can share knowledge via such media as Facebook, it is easy to confuse opinion, information and knowledge. One can assert anything as fact. And when these assertions are short, simply stated and not defended carefully, they oversimplify a complex world. Facebook postings, blogs, message boards, texts: We are awash in ungrounded opinion masquerading as information and even knowledge. The world is flat; the moon landing was fake; Obama was born in Kenya; HIV doesn't exist. This is dangerous stuff, and it is difficult for people to sift through.

And sometimes having more valid information about a problem can lead to greater psychological distress, as Cotten et al. (2011) discovered in their research on Internet searches for medical information. Many are familiar with looking up symptoms on the Internet and then concluding that they have a grave disease! On the other hand, people can effectively self-treat by gathering Internet information and not having to rely on experts. This is not a clear picture yet.

Why are Americans so prone to post one-liners on FB and then respond with "like"? There are several reasons:

- Using smartphones promotes brief hunting-and-pecking, not the composition of complex sentences with conditional clauses.
- It is easier to think small and short, rather than to take a big-picture view.
- People are in a hurry, and post on the run.
- Posting, texting, tweeting are viewed not really as literary acts, as writing, but as chatting, almost as oral expression.
- Brief, acronym- and emoticon-laden expression (e.g., LOL, ☺) is simply easier for people who don't want to labor over careful composition, remembering whether they can split infinitives or end sentences with prepositions.

Ours is a **post-textual age**, in which images and abbreviations stand in for traditional writing. Post-textual expression is nearly oral, as text messaging is a kind of talking. **Chatting** refers to synchronous online communication, for example conducted in chat rooms, that resembles face-to-face chatting at cocktail parties or over lunch. Chatting is sociable, but it risks trivializing what I am calling discourse—considered reflection turned into speech or writing. Americans chat endlessly, trading opinions masquerading as fact. We are sociable people, but, regrettably, we are rather anti-intellectual. We inhabit a bumper-sticker culture, which we now transact online.

Even an hour of television watched or websites visited can transform us into an instant expert. We now think we understand the economy, war, parenting, divorce, sports. We can sound knowledgeable, even though we have just scratched the surface. There is so much "surface" everywhere, at our fingertips. There is simply too much information, much of it misleading, and precious little real knowledge. Oversharers share trivia or falsehoods.

It is good that amateurs can educate themselves using the Internet and release themselves from dependence on experts. However, to become really expert we must delve below the surface, precisely as experts learn to do. The ability to distinguish between sheer opinion and knowledge is learned, not innate. When we are experts, we quickly learn to make these distinctions. Laypeople can become experts through long study. This is the promise of democratic knowledge shared widely.

Online vs. face-to-face?

I argued that people overshare when communicating electronically in ways that they wouldn't if face-to-face. Embarrassment prevents them from saying things that they might text or tweet. This is good; we need to keep some of our private thoughts to ourselves. A pornographic public sphere reveals everything that is personal and private, including our sexuality. It is difficult to have friends, or stay friends, when we disclose everything. It could be said that drama, discussed earlier, is saying too much, leading to hurt feelings.

Instead of condemning online interaction, I pose a distinction between sharing and oversharing, friendship based on protecting private thoughts and letting it all hang out. This distinguishing allows us to rethink the dichotomy of online friends and "real" face-to-face friendships. One can overshare in both situations, and one can refrain from oversharing. People on Facebook probably have more FB "friends" than real face-to-face friends, but some of their FB friends are also intimate friends with whom they interact frequently. The closer the friendship, the safer one feels sharing intimate thoughts. One can imagine these friendships and even love affairs deepened by online interaction, especially when distance intervenes to make face-to-face interaction impossible.

Consider lovers separated by travel or commuting. Using the Internet is perfect for staying in touch. Oversharing is not the same as intimacy. Intimacy is sharing based on trust. Lovers trust each other not to judge inner thoughts and feelings. Oversharing occurs between people who may not be in love or who are not bonded by trust. People feel they can overshare because there won't be emotional accountability, the way there would be between lovers. Indeed, oversharing may be a strategy to become intimate, a way for men to appear sensitive and for women to appear sexually open. As we will discuss below, there is Internet-dating code for this type of sexuality, such as "adventurous" and "open-minded." Those mean kinky, as we will see. And men say they are seeking their "soul mate," even if they just want to get laid. If only women and men didn't live on different planets!

And so no one exists purely face-to-face or purely online, except perhaps the World of Warcraft gamer who never sees the sun rise or set. Most people live offline and online lives. Before we could express ourselves online and via texting, there was less oversharing and more genuine interaction. The boundary between public and private was clearer. I want it to become clear again, which is why I examine the boundary between offline (public) and online (private) interactions. If there is advice to be derived from this, perhaps this is it:

- If you can call, call and don't text.
- If you can meet, meet and don't call or text.
- Don't say things to people online or via texting that you wouldn't say to their faces.
- Use electronic communication for utilitarian purposes, to set a time to meet for a movie. It is OK to write love letters, but save emotional expressiveness for face-to-face interaction.
- Don't allow pornographic communication to replace face-to-face sexuality and intimacy.
- Don't become a slave to text messaging, such that one is always in a conversation that doesn't seem to quit.
- When you text or compose email, pretend that you are writing a letter or a memo. Use full sentences, punctuation, and proper grammar.
- Don't exaggerate in order to enhance yourself.

This is social etiquette for the Internet age! We need to live life offscreen and to protect the public/private boundary. There are some things that shouldn't be said, especially casually. We all need and seek intimacy, and the best kind of intimacy depends on the adoring gaze, the hug, the kiss, the tender word. Sex broadcast over webcams is objectifying and unrewarding, for the most part. In our increasingly pornographic culture, there are no secrets, no privacy, no downtime. We need to work hard to change that, beginning with the ways in which we present ourselves on the screen and in person.

DISCUSSION QUESTIONS

1. Why is Facebook so addictive?! Do you know many people not on Facebook?
2. Does Facebook help you form a community of like-minded friends and do these friendships carry over into your face-to-face world?
3. Is posting online (e.g., tweeting) a form of narcissism or is this a legitimate and useful form of self-revelation?

IV: Online Dating

"I love you, let's meet" reflects the quandary of dating electronically.

Internet dating is all about **framing**, constructing oneself for the opposite (or same) sex (see Goffman 1974). One frames by selecting photos of oneself carefully, to best advantage. One is in control of the information about oneself that one shares. There is not complete plasticity; the 60-year-old cannot readily lose 40 years of wrinkle lines. But the 45-year-old can easily become 40, and the portly person can become "athletic," as the terminology goes. And one's interests can be as varied and as altruistic as one wants.

We will see that men and women frame differently, largely because their aims are different in pursuing online dating. This overgeneralizes; many women and men want the same things and use similar means to attain it. And many people don't spin the truth about themselves. They are genuine and honest about who they are. But, by and large, there is a good deal of selectivity involved in framing, largely because our high divorce rate leaves many people in their 40s and 50s without partners but with kids and mortgages. One of the central symptoms of an anomic society is the glut of divorced people looking for partners, sex, something.

Virginia Vitzthum (2007) in her excellent book *I Love You, Let's Meet*, on the Internet dating scene, notes that such dating is easy and efficient, if unsatisfying. Online dating is a meet/meat market, much like a bar but with a vaster array of opportunities. One can spend all day and night logged on to the relevant dating site, ever in pursuit of something new and different. One gets home from a date and immediately goes online looking for someone else. Much like speed dating, one can go through many options quickly, without having to hang out at a bar inhaling second-hand smoke.

Oversharing is an almost automatic outcome of this kind of electronic dating. Frequently, many messages, emails, and texts are exchanged before the first meeting. One can spill one's gut about values, the past, sexual preferences. One has already posted a detailed profile with a rich array of such information: age, race, height, weight, the type of relationship one seeks (e.g., casual, committed), income, political and religious preference, number of dependents, marital status, personality type, sexual kinks, hobbies, ideas of an ideal first date, etc. Oversharing begins the minute one walks into the electronic bar of the dating service.

This may simplify things—if people didn't frame, spin and outright lie. Body type and age are frequently identified as characteristics about which people lie. A woman I know said she had trouble admitting that she was 40. There are euphemisms for fat, such as BBW—big beautiful woman. Frequently, people post flattering photos that don't convey what they look like in everyday life, or that are from ten years ago. Men post photos of themselves without shirts on and they may send photos of their erections. Yes, I am often ashamed of my gender! Women, too, may send pornographic photos, recognizing that their value to men is largely sexual.

Men Want Sex, Women Want Men

Internet dating is gendered; women and men approach it differently. Although sites such as Match.com appear to arrange marriages, many men who pursue online dating are seeking sex and are often married or in relationships. Many women are seeking relationships, and they are frequently divorced. Women receive hundreds of inquiries (messages, emails), and men generally do the pursuing. This is just like "real" life! But on dating sites, men must appear to want relationships, seeking their "soul mates."

Dating sites flourish because people seek relationships, including sex but also including traditional romance. We are a society in which people are alone together, Durkheim's egoism and Marx's estrangement. We are especially needy because many adults get divorced and then are too busy and encumbered with children and other responsibilities to live a single person's dating life. They can't go to bars or singles functions. Dating online is efficient, under their control, and gives them many options.

There are now even sites, such as Ashley Madison (ashleymadison.com), not earmarked for single people (although AM allows singles). Their advertising slogan is "Life is short. Have an affair." They are enticing married people and people in committed relationships to cheat on their partners. AM facilitates this kind of matching, for a fee of course. That's the other side of the popularity of dating and sex sites: call it the **commercialization of love and sex**. Most of these sites charge a fee, and we willingly pay it because we are needy and because of the other efficiencies noted above.

Increasingly, everything is commercialized, and most goods and services are available online. Dating and sex sites are different, though, in that we—people themselves—are the product. And we in a sense manufacture ourselves by framing, spinning and sometimes outright lying about our demographics and about our aims and goals.

Perhaps this is true of all marketing (advertising), as we learn to put our best foot forward. An auto manufacturer that produces a car with less-than-ideal crash test ratings won't disclose this willingly. It may actually downplay such ratings, arguing that they are bogus. Similarly, the obese and inactive dating-site player won't term himself obese, but instead embraces acronyms. There is nothing inherently wrong with shorthand. As commodities ourselves, we should control what information we put out there.

Even a casual glance at dating sites and their personal profiles reveals a huge amount of oversharing, especially on women's profile pages. There is incredible length and detail devoted to exactly who the person is, and what they are seeking. Interestingly, people often include prohibitions or turn-offs, much as they are highly selective when purchasing a car or a pair of shoes. They want partners between 46 and 54; non-smokers only; nobody with kids. They won't date men who have their abs displayed in their photo! (A reasonable decision, that.) They want only religious partners, or partners who are at least 5 foot 11 inches. I am struck by how many women want male partners taller than they are, sometimes much taller. There must be something about dominance and masculinity going on.

And men, predictably, want younger women, just as some younger men want **cougars**, older, more sexually experienced, perhaps needier women. A whole dating and mating vernacular has sprung up, complete with clever acronyms: **BBW**, **SWF**, **NSA**, **MILF**. I define all of these terms in my glossary, but I will only define part of the last acronym; the reader can guess the rest! In economic terms, the dating market—it is a market after all—is increasingly segmented, with consumers savvy about what they are looking for in the way of particular profiles and preferences.

Men pursue women on dating sites, much as they do in the offline world. Attractive women receive many inquiries from interested men. They often don't reply if they are not interested. There are few manners in play here. Men are similarly unmannered when they introduce themselves by saying "Hey, baby" or when they send unclothed photos right away. There is little spelling, grammar or syntax in electronic chatter, no less in Internet dating. There are also few real writers. People traffic in phrases and single sentences, but rarely in paragraphs.

This would seem to be the opposite of oversharing—this economy of words. But in our post-textual era, the "text" is the photos, both clothed and naked, that often follow quickly after the first contact. The photos are the real text, the all-important initial visuals. This is exactly like a bar, although in a bar or club the gaze is quickly followed by inescapable conversation. One can exchange very few words in online dating before one winds up in bed, or perhaps even in love. The exchange of photos constitutes over-sharing, although some people, probably in their 40s and 50s, really write as a way of getting to know each other. I know of a case where a highly literary guy, recently divorced, wrote many revealing letters and love letters to a younger woman, who said she was turned off by the "pressure" that this constituted. In other words, she didn't want verbal intimacy.

For men to do the pursuing perpetuates traditional gender roles. They pursue on those dating sites where everyone has access to everyone else's profile. On sites such as Match (match.com) and eHarmony (eharmony.com), the matching is done by the website. Couples are introduced, based on perceived commonalities between their profiles, backgrounds, interests. This certainly reduces the "supply" of potential partners. And it erases the role of **serendipity**, the sheer accident of romantic attraction, which may occur between seemingly unmatchable and different partners.

Self-Framing: Women who Like Baseball and Men who Seek Soul Mates

The framing of oneself in the dating profile anticipates a certain reading by other daters, with women wanting to appear feminine and submissive, and men sensitive and compassionate. Some women will highlight their desire for a traditional relationship, with the man calling the shots. Or they will say they are sexually submissive, transplanting gender roles into the bedroom. They might also indicate that they like baseball and other male sports, even if this might contradict their femininity. It is submissive for women to claim a false interest in sports because they are subordinating who they really are in order to please the man. Some women may actually like sports and be athletes, such as runners or triathletes, themselves. There is a fine line to be walked by women who want to appear feminine but also to appeal to men who like "guy" things. Indeed, it is ingenious to signal one's femininity by appearing to submit to men's direction, interests, and hobbies.

Every woman alive knows that every man wants one thing and only one thing—sex! And so men construct their profiles to appear empathetic, caring, and relationship-oriented. Men frequently indicate that they are looking for soul mates, women with whom to take long walks and talk over intimate matters such as personal philosophies and interior decoration. As women seek to be feminine as well as sexual, and above all not too high maintenance, men seek to have a feminine side and not just to want to get laid. Women don't want to appear to be bitches, and men don't want to seem to be looking for sex instead of relationships.

We are all prisoners of gender in these senses. Ideally, women would not care so much about seeming feminine and non-demanding, and men could genuinely seek fulfilling relationships. We all play **gender roles**, enacting our sexual identity (e.g., male, female) in socially appropriate ways. The problem is that there is not universal agreement on what these roles should be. With the sixties and post-sixties women's movement and women's rapid labor force entry, women are allowed to be more like men in their occupational aspirations, even if, contradictorily, they are still expected to be lady-like in the bedroom (or a combination of lady-like and kinky, as I discuss in the pornography chapter).

Many people on dating sites are not single, even if they claim to be. They are looking for affairs. A significant number of them seem to be coming out of repressive marriages and they are enjoying their newfound freedom and experimenting sexually. The term "adventurous" is also used to create the same impression.

There can be a great deal of heartache if women begin dating men they thought were single but who are really married. This is not purely an Internet phenomenon, although online dating promotes deception simply by giving people the opportunity to frame themselves. How many men will volunteer that they are married when they are on a dating site? A few, certainly, but probably not most. And women can be married, too, and find themselves on dating sites. But the vast majority of women tell the truth about their marital status, while men are more tempted to lie about theirs. This is because the men are not seeking a real relationship, but only sex, while the women, who are single or divorced, genuinely want a long-term relationship—**LTR**!

Are men by nature polygamous? Perhaps. However, it has been estimated that only about a third of Americans commit infidelity (Laumann et al. 1994: 590–96). We tend to exaggerate extramarital affairs because they are so often publicized in our culture, much as we may tend to believe that everyone engages in the kinky activities depicted in some porn videos and films. Our differing gender expectations may greatly influence the ways in which men and women view sex and relationships differently, with women much more likely than men to link sex and love. Whether this is because of our different sexual natures or because of our **gender socialization**, I am not sure. I am certain that most men and most women view sex and relationships differently, a fact that plays out in the ways in which women and men construct their online dating profiles.

Men, who are said to be "visual," may not actually read the women's profiles but instead just look at their photos. Women may do the same thing to men. It could be that men and women are converging in that they both view dating as a commercialized, appearance-driven activity in which the outer shell is more important than what goes on inside. Dating sites encourage this because they offer so many options. If Tuesday's date wasn't perfect, one can go out with a different person on Wednesday. And so on. The supply is nearly limitless.

The limitless supply creates a restless, never-satisfied consumer. People date serially, trading in one model for the upgrade. "I like to meet new people" becomes the mantra. Variety trumps quality and commitment. This is perhaps what happens when love and sex become commodities, to be traded in the online marketplace. Everyone is degraded, reduced to their profile and especially their profile photo.

In the pornography chapter, I discuss the way in which we reveal all of ourselves in a culture that has nearly eliminated privacy. In online dating, the pornographic photos are the ones we send after first contact has been established, based on a clothed profile photo (unless we are dealing with sex sites such as AdultFriendFinders, where one can be nude from the beginning). Men sometimes post shirtless photos and soon thereafter send photos of their erections—a practice that Martian anthropologists would dissect with great interest! But women, too, enter the fray by sending nude photos, including of their genital areas, which, these days, are often shaved (another tidbit for future social scientists). There is a traffic in bodies that occurs frantically underneath the surface of the Internet dating sites. We can use the site itself to send these revealing photos, or we can use email or just text them. Above, I discussed "sexting," of which this is an example. But here the purpose is to raise our value in the dating market, indicating the quality of our bodies and our sexual adventurousness.

I am convinced that in this pornographic culture, such self-revelation has become mainstream—the norm, as we sociologists say. One might wonder how this could be true when over 90 percent of Americans claim to be religious. Perhaps taboos on sexuality imposed by religion become all the more enticing, also explaining why 40-somethings coming out of sexless and conventional marriages want to bust loose and explore bondage, domination/submission, and swinging. Forbidden fruit, and all that.

This is a combustible mix: online dating and an overtly sexualized culture in which pornographic representation and self-representation are common. How else do we explain the erection photographs that men post and send? The Martian anthropologist examining these strange engorged members would probably conclude that there is little variation; they all look similar, with some a bit longer and thicker than others. They would conclude that penis size is a marker of masculinity, and they might also conclude that women, too, believe that size matters. It certainly does for women in the breast department. The Martians would wonder why some women have artificial implants and others do not. Finally, they might wonder why the media are chock full of advertisements for medications that address sexual dysfunction.

Erection Photographs but Erectile Dysfunction

Craigslist is not exactly a dating site, although one can date using CL, as it is termed. CL is now viewed as notorious because a man named Philip Markoff killed a woman masseuse/escort who advertised on the site. Markoff later committed suicide in prison. But CL is free and widely available. It is also geographically focused, so one can find people in the same town and region. One can find traditional dating on CL, men seeking women and vice versa, for possible long-term relationships. But one can also find casual and kinky hook-ups of all types: two people, three people, more people. Men on men, women on women. It is a full menu.

The Martian anthropologist would read these ads with great interest. They reveal much about American sexuality. The people seeking casual and kinky hook-ups are explicit in what they want. A second guy to have sex with one's wife while he watches. A couple that wants to swap with other couples. A woman seeking a guy who likes 420 (marijuana). People who like to "party"—drink and use drugs. And, frequently, singles and couples post sexually explicit photos of themselves having sex and of their naked genitals. A quick tour of CL's casual-sex offerings will expose more erections than any Martian will ever see in one place!

The erection has become iconic for many Americans. Men display it proudly, as a sign of their identity. Some women seek guys who are proud to be pictured erect. It is said that some women like big ones, although most women I know care less about this part than about the brain and the heart. But, as I said, we inhabit a **sexualized culture**, in which images of sexuality and sexualized bodies have become commonplace, available to anyone with a laptop or smartphone. Their images are everywhere on the Internet: advertising, dating sites, fashion, magazines, and Craigslist. My kids, late teenagers, may have seen more sexuality and sexual bodies than I have; it is nearly impossible to look away.

If women's breasts dominated sexual iconography during the fifties and sixties, the erection dominates contemporary culture. Breasts haven't disappeared; they still signify a certain femininity and female sexuality. Implants and plastic surgery abound. But breasts are inanimate; one can lift them and enhance them, but they are not everyday accomplishments in the way that erections are. One is not automatically fully engorged unless the libido is firing. The erection, for many men, is what they produce publicly for the perusal and evaluation of women and perhaps, secretly, of other men.

With high blood pressure, too much drinking and the general stress of living, the erection is increasingly difficult to achieve. This strikes to the heart of masculinity, requiring Viagra as a counterpart to the iconic image of the erection. If the failure to achieve full arousal is a body problem for many men, the medical solution is to medicate the problem. Online dating, a body industry involving traffic in bodies, requires men with erectile dysfunction (ED), as it is called, to seek pharmaceutical assistance. I am not minimizing the pain of ED, for in stable relationships it can wreak havoc. But erections are not just erections anymore; they are public symbols of private masculinity—the ability to get and stay hard.

There is a female counterpart to the erection, which in a sense replaces the earlier centrality of Marilyn Monroe-like cleavage and breasts. This is the shaved genital area. Indeed, many women and men under 40 shave their genital areas, perhaps to make sexual photos more graphic. In the case of women, a quick tour of Craigslist finds far fewer women than men who post naked pictures when seeking partners, including kinky partners. The naked representations of women on Craigslist occur primarily where the women are part of a couple, seeking either other couples for a foursome or single men or women for the two different kinds of threesomes (MFM or FFM, in the lingo).

But I have an additional theory about women who shave. They exhibit a child-like and prepubescent sexuality, enhancing the impression that the women so portrayed are submissive to dominant men. These may well be the same women who enjoy kinky sex. Sociologists recognize that these practices become norms, the standards for others who may not think twice about the meaning of shaving their private parts. After all, in our culture of oversharing, there are no more private parts; everything is on view.

DISCUSSION QUESTIONS

1. Is online dating pathetic or a definite improvement over meeting romantic partners in a crowded, smoky bar?

2. Is it human nature to spin one's profile and photo into the most desirable package or does the Internet call forth a certain deception in the ways people present themselves to possible romantic partners?

3. Do photographs of naked bodies and body parts reduce the person to his or her outer shell or is this a form of sexual and human liberation, where people are unashamed of their bodies and their sexuality?

V: Internet Pornography

⭕‹×›⭕

How can we explain the fact that at least half of Internet activity involves sexual images and stories?

I have already introduced the concept of a pornographic public sphere, a culture in which people have no secrets and everything is laid bare. Here, we consider bare bodies, as we have begun to do in our discussion of online dating. We have noticed that people who use online dating sites, including Craigslist, traffic in amateur pornographic self-representation, especially of their erections and their shaved parts. By pornographic culture I mean a culture of all oversharing, but especially the kind of oversharing represented by pornography and the naked profile photos found on certain dating sites. Pornography functions here both as a metaphor for oversharing and as a literal kind of oversharing—the oversharing of the sexual activity that many men and some women view on the Internet and in videos. Although we have few systematic data on how many people watch porn, a recent Australian survey finds that 30 percent of women admit to watching porn as compared to 70 percent of men who watch (Lee 2010).

The Internet has mainstreamed pornography, which is found everywhere. An August 11, 2011 Google search of the single word "pornography" reveals no fewer than 48,900,000 results. It would take days to wade through all of these options. In this chapter, I focus on a single free porn site found at www.youporn.com. By free site I am referring to a porn site that doesn't require a payment from the user, although at youporn.com one is offered the pay-for-view option of watching the full-length video instead of a free clip lasting about 3–20 minutes. The site is a window on our strange world, a world that would astonish the Martian anthropologists!

Videos for Every Fetish

The youporn.com site offers fully 61 categories of porn videos collected from other porn sites, from masturbation to group sex to interviews (where the woman being interviewed for a job has sex with the interviewer). Most of the categories are **kinky**, that is, outside mainstream sexual activity. But any sociologist, whether Martian or earthling, would regard the concept of kinky as highly relative, sexually, ethically, and personally. Many seemingly respectable adults like to engage in bondage, domination/submission, swinging, web-camming. Many Americans identify themselves as **bicurious**, meaning they want to try sex with a member of their sex, possibly with their heterosexual spouse or partner present. The cultural relativity of kinkiness makes a discussion of pornography less straightforward than many would like. What is pornographic, kinky, and fetishistic depends on the personal standards being applied.

And so I use the term "kinky" loosely, implying that church-goers in the Midwest or South might be offended by the discussion and especially portrayal of these activities. That does not mean that conservative and religious people don't watch porn or engage in these kinky behaviors. Indeed, I suspect that the more a person's religion and morality place taboos on certain sexual behaviors, the more enticing those behaviors become; they are forbidden fruit. Less repressed people might be less tempted by these fruits because they have done them before and can take them or leave them; they are no big deal. Indeed, most baby boomers like me, born somewhere between 1947 and 1960, have experimented sexually and there is a sense among many of us that "sex is just sex." Most of it conducted between consenting adults is all good or at least morally permissible.

Let me put my cards squarely on the table. I don't watch porn; I don't engage in **role playing**, especially acting out the roles of dominant partner and submissive partner. This is not to say that I am conservative sexually; I am non-judgmental about what others do. **Sexual libertarianism** is the opposite of what Alan Dershowitz (1998), the Harvard civil-liberties lawyer, terms **sexual McCarthyism**, a repressive attitude toward sexual self-expression that places a high value on traditional sexuality between married partners. I don't think that much, if anything, should be illegal in the way of sexual behavior between consenting adults. Indeed, I believe that we would be freed from many anxieties and neuroses about sex—especially guilt—if we were less proscriptive and more tolerant of sexual exploration. Everyone remembers what happens when schools ban certain books, such as the very tame *Catcher in the Rye*, by J.D. Salinger (1951). We teenagers would all go out and read the books, thumbing through them for the dirty parts. Make something illegal or immoral and we tempt people to try it, even if trying it produces significant conflicts for them as their religion and morality clash with their libertine behavior. We do not ban something because it is evil; rather, it is evil because we ban it.

Having said all this, it is still highly notable that men post erection photos on dating sites and that porn sites, which offer every conceivable variety of kinky video, are so heavily trafficked. There is something going on which requires explaining. In the previous chapter, I suggested that the image of the erection suggests successful accomplishment of masculinity and that is why guys will post numerous shots of their erect penises without posting a single facial shot. And now we have a nation of pornographers, of men who watch and produce porn and of women who star in porn videos.

There are two types of pornography, **professional porn** and **amateur porn**.

Professional porn involves paid actors and actresses who have sex for money and get filmed while doing it. These videos are purchased for home use or sampled for a fee online. Amateur porn is porn people can make at home or at parties and then post on the web. This has become a huge enterprise, judging by the number of amateur porn sites available. And the porn videos on these sites seem to change daily, as amateurs—perhaps your neighbors!—submit their video wares.

Why do we like to watch people have sex and to be watched by others? Sex fascinates us, partly because it is taboo in some circles. As well, revealing everything about our private lives has become a feature of our (as I am calling it) pornographic public sphere—a sphere in which nothing is held back. This is partly a remedy for boredom and anomie, I suspect, a way to fill the time. And everyone wants and needs sex, although there are certainly variations in their outlets and their libidinal needs. We even have a new quasi-medical term for the person who can't get enough sex: **sex addict**. I am dubious about this term for several reasons. First, is this really an addiction, an irresistible compulsion, like alcohol and cigarettes? Second, we members of the male gender think about sex a lot; it comes with the territory of being male. Are we all sex addicts? Third, to call something an addiction may remove some of the responsibility for the behavior from the person, and I'm not sure that people are truly compelled to want sex, and more sex, 24/7. Many of us love sex, but we compartmentalize it, much as we compartmentalize going for a run or watching TV.

Perhaps the deepest reason why we consume and even "act" in pornography of an amateur kind is to become porn stars. This also explains the popularity of the television shows *Dancing with the Stars* and *American Idol* and indeed other reality television, such as the show *Survivor*. We want to be stars because our own lives are humdrum. And sex is fun. And anyone can learn to webcam and video themselves and others having sex.

Why the fetishes, the specific lists of non-traditional sexual behavior featured in many porn videos? Because for repressed and religious people, sex is taboo and hence enticing, the argument I made earlier. We aren't fetishistic by nature, born to like feet, submitting, and swinging. We learn these tastes, much as we learn to prefer hamburgers to Italian or Italian to sushi. Or we may like everything presented to us in the smorgasbord of diverse sexualities—the gangbangs, threesomes, job interviews, swapping partners with the neighbors. Fetishes spice up a boring sex life, even if we experience them vicariously by watching the many varieties of videos offered.

I do not share the view that pornography of most sorts triggers violence against women. But a remarkable number of porn videos seem to portray women as submissive and men as dominant. I have heard it said that strong, professional-on-the-outside women go home and want to be "feminine" and submissive in the bedroom. I suspect that few professionally successful women, with multiple academic degrees, become girlish in bed. This is a male fantasy designed to turn the political tables on women who work alongside men and even sometimes become their bosses. Men can render them submissive sexually by having their way with them, talking degradingly to them, tying them up, pulling their hair, and spanking their asses. Again, this is a male fantasy, as so much of pornography seems to be.

Women watch porn, too, as I just indicated, and women make and act in porn videos, especially of the amateur kind. One finds videos with women seemingly behaving submissively. Women gaze at naked men just as men gaze at naked women. But porn is heavily gendered, with men doing most of the watching and men engaging in most of the dominant behavior on screen. One of the videos offered involves the interview situation, as I remarked. This is quite telling: The male pretends to be interviewing and auditioning the obviously younger woman for a job in the porn industry. He tells her that she needs to be seen to take direction. He tells her to strip, and sometimes the woman is reluctant. He tells her that she must strip if she wants to act in porn videos. Once she is naked, he asks her to bend over and reveal herself fully, much like in a prison search scenario. This is degrading, and he is exhibiting his domination. After requiring her to have oral sex with him, he then proceeds to have sex with her, usually of the unprotected kind. The inside story is that he is not really casting for porn videos but simply deceiving these degraded young women, who are lured into having sex with a complete stranger who videotapes their every move.

These interview videos are emblematic of a culture in which people bare all and women submit to men, who live out their fantasies of domination on the screen. In each video, the stripping and sex are preceded by a few minutes of chatting, as he pretends to get to know his interviewee. It is striking how demure these women are, how willing to please, even when they have reservations. Some even allow him to ejaculate in them without being on birth control. And only a few apparently insist that he wear a condom, reducing the risk of HIV. I got mad watching these videos—mad at my gender, mad at women who submit, mad at the people who routinely watch the videos. I clicked on "interview" videos because I couldn't imagine what these entailed. The group sex videos speak for themselves.

Both rational-choice theorists and postmodernists reject Marx's view that people have **false consciousness**—a distorted view of the world and of their own best interests and needs. False consciousness is provoked by **ideologies** that fundamentally deceive people, such as the ideas of male supremacy over women. However, false consciousness perfectly explains why women shave and submit and why men get off on porn. We are taught by our culture to want things and engage in behaviors that are unhealthy for us. By whose standard? By the standard of the rational person, the thinker, the theorist. How do we know these standards? Habermas (1984, 1987), following Plato, suggests we can know the truth through rational thought and debate, what he calls the **ideal speech situation**, involving speech unconstrained by bullying and lying and governed by acknowledgement of the power of the strongest argument. I *know* that pornographic male dominance, especially bondage, is bad for everyone, both the doers and the watchers. Tying people up during sex enacts a rape fantasy.

The Pornographic Prism

Presumably, the young women in the interview videos are being paid in order to allow their videos to be posted on the Internet, even if they are not receiving the $1,000 to $5,000 that he says they will make daily in the "adult" film industry. But amateur porn is abundant and deserves notice. These are willing couples and groups who film themselves and post their porn on amateur sites. Amateurs also "cam" themselves having sex live. Amateurs might charge a fee to view their wares, or to watch their camming, but by and large amateurs are not full-time actors in the porn industry. And many of them get off simply by being watched.

The boundaries around amateur porn are blurry. People who post nude photos on Internet dating sites are pornographers, as are people who text naked photos or email them as attachments. Sexting is pornography. The Craigslist erection photos are porn. It could be argued that wearing revealing clothes is pornographic, with exhibitionism inviting a voyeuristic response. Victoria's Secret purveys porn, as does the tellingly named restaurant/bar chain called Hooters.

I term the various ways in which we, viewers of porn, position ourselves as pornographic subjects, whether we appear on screen or not, the **pornographic prism**. This refers to the way we imagine ourselves enacting the roles played on the porn screen and then produce that image in our own amateur videos, our dress, our discourse, our bedroom behavior. We star in the porn videos of our own lives, seeking the glamour and exposure of the well-known stars and other amateur actors such as the submissive young women having sex while being interviewed. Watching pornography is an imagining of oneself having the varied sex viewed on the screen. Inevitably, it falls short because we are watching others cavort.

This prism reveals sexual subjects having sex in the many ways identified by the porn site mentioned above. We can see ourselves through this prism as we dress, talk, and act the part. We learn how to have sex through this pornographic prism, which provides a sex education of sorts. Most high-school boys watch porn, and they learn sex this way. Is this realistic sex? That depends on whether their would-be sexual partners view themselves through the pornographic prism, with men dominating women and women behaving submissively.

The feminist critique of pornography as objectifying women is, in my view, close to the mark but misses it. It is not that women are being represented as sexual objects for the delight of men; after all, women in many porn videos are active agents who seem to be enjoying what they are doing. Rather, pornography depicts women as submissive and men as dominant, reproducing gender roles at play in the larger society. Although this is not always the case, I have seen very few porn videos made from the woman's point of view or by a feminist woman director. Porn is a male-dominated industry catering to male fantasies of dominance, control, younger women, multiple partners and the centrality of the erection, discussed above.

The Slovenian theorist Žižek (2006) views porn as conservative:

> Pornography is, and it is, a deeply conservative genre. It's not a genre where everything is permitted. It's a genre based on a fundamental prohibition. We cross one threshold, you can see everything, close ups and so on, but the price you pay for it is that the narrative which justifies sexual activity should not be taken seriously. The screenwriters for pornography cannot be so stupid. You know, these vulgar narratives of a housewife alone at home, a plumber comes, fixes the hole, then the housewife turns to him, "Sorry, but I have another hole to be fixed. Can you do it?" or whatever. Obviously there is some kind of a censorship here. You have either an emotionally engaging film, but then you should stop bust before showing it all, sexual act, or you can see it all but you are now allowed then to be emotionally seriously engaged. So that's the tragedy of pornography.

And there is another interesting feature of most heterosexual pornography: It has a bisexual subtext, where women have sex with other women, men join other men in group sex (but without having male-on-male sex), and men, having sex with only one woman, display their erections for the viewing pleasure of other men. Given that male professional porn actors are often well-endowed, one would assume that there would be several levels of discomfort here: The male viewer feels inadequate; he feels weird watching other men have sex; he feels deprived of the sex they are getting.

Žižek (2005) comments on the role of men in heterosexual porn:

> Pornography is a genre where you would think everything is permitted. No! It's the most codified of genres. But this, for me, is its ultimate charm. I spoke with a Hollywood pornography producer, who told me that he deliberately stages the action so that the male viewer doesn't identify with the guy doing the fucking. He's just a machine. You, the viewer, want to be convinced that the woman is addressing you. And the deepest fantasy is that the ultimate woman—the femme fatale—would be a drag queen, a dressed-up man.

Indeed, the pornographic prism, which reduces people to sexualized bodies cavorting on the screen, is based on the experience of deprivation: If one had one's way, one would be having sex, not just watching it. Indeed, some people have sex with porn playing in the background, perhaps getting them in the mood but perhaps also transporting them onto a pornographic ground on which they become players alongside the people they are viewing.

Viewing people, and oneself, through this prism transforms sex into a spectator sport. After all, we are a nation of watchers, not doers. To be sure, some people "do": They bike, run, use the elliptical. Others "do" by making amateur porn. But even this porn is to be watched by others who seek to inhabit the same ground of sexual bodies.

There is a certain anonymity to porn. Personality takes a backseat to body, especially to sex organs. Anyone could play the parts.

In each and every porn video, the ending is predictable. The actors get there in different ways, but eventually it all blurs and it feels like watching one long, complicated video, in installments. There is a bit of talking, perhaps some foreplay, intercourse, orgasms, perhaps a bit more talking. This is a thin plot, but it must be very compelling to the many who surf the nearly 49 million porn sites. Through the pornographic prism we are only our bodies, a disembodiment that is quite dehumanizing.

Another interpretation of the pornographic prism is that people, especially men, are living their fantasies vicariously. But where do we get these fantasies? From a pornographic culture in which men enjoy two women, people tie each other up, they spank and pull hair, they have sex during the job interview. Perhaps we all seek to explore sexually, but are the kinky video categories in our DNA? I am tempted to believe that people experiment early in life, realize they have done it all (or most of it) and come to realize that sex is just sex and that sex is better with love.

That is not to identify sex and love completely. The problem with that equation is that it suggests to teenagers that they must be in love in order to experiment sexually. Teenagers have children, get married, follow each other to college. It also implies that people who have sex while in love are actually "making love," where they are simply having playful sex in order to gratify each other and themselves. Victorians have brainwashed us that we must be in love to have sex and that sex and love are identical. One might simply observe that people in committed relationships have better sex than do strangers because they like and respect each other and learn each other's moves.

All Sex, All the Time

The Martian anthropologist mentioned earlier would observe that humans spend a great deal of time and money on sex. We seem to have sex on our brains, as our Internet porn preoccupation would suggest. Our television shows are sexual; advertising is sexual; clothing is sexual. And we use rapid information and communication technologies to communicate about sex—phone sex, sexting, camming, Internet hook-ups, pornography.

Does this represent a healthy lifting of previous Puritanical prohibitions against sex? Or does it signify an unhealthy obsession with the erasure of the boundary between the public and the personal? I would favor the first explanation, except that the pornographic prism involves watching and being watched, not doing. As I said, viewing sex through the pornographic prism falls short, even if one masturbates while watching. Perhaps it is useful to imagine oneself in sexual exploration, releasing one from Puritanism. But that would not explain the omnipresence of porn in our culture.

One could conclude that what is at stake is not sex but the imagining of a different, better life. Sex here stands for utopia, the good society, in which there is no pain or deprivation. The pornographic prism reveals people unburdened by the restraints of bourgeois morality. They play for its own sake. This reinterpretation of Freud's concept of the libido as Eros, the life instinct, is consistent with Herbert Marcuse's arguments in his (1955) *Eros and Civilization* about people liberated from bourgeois morality. He reinterprets Freud's concept of **sex drive** as **life instinct**—a yearning for happiness, gratification, and the avoidance of pain.

I am hesitant to condemn pornography both because sex is good (compared to war!) and because the **sexualization** of our culture is telling us something: People are not satisfied with their lives, including, but not limited to, their sex lives. They seek intimacy, fraternity, community, meaning. Now sampling the many varieties of kinky porn videos is not the route to salvation, especially if people go broke paying for the privilege of watching others cavort. But our porn- and sex-crazed culture can be read as a culture in which people seek to unify their minds and bodies (this also explains people's yearning to exercise).

The problem with porn is threefold: It is not real sex, person-to-person. It is enjoyed only vicariously. To be sure, one can masturbate while watching it, but this is a solitary activity. Two people can watch porn and enjoy sex together, but they quickly turn their attention to each other. Second, porn involves self-revelation of a kind that blurs the boundary between personal and public, providing a metaphor for what I call a pornographic public sphere in which everyone knows everything about everyone. Third, in much porn men dominate women, who submit, all in the name of role playing.

DISCUSSION QUESTIONS

1. Why is porn so controversial? People love it or hate it.
2. Why do people, especially men, watch so much porn? Is this healthy or a symptom that something is wrong with our society?
3. Can a society that deemphasizes porn still liberate people sexually? Or is porn sexually liberating?

VI: A Non-Pornographic Public Sphere

Sharing is necessary for intimacy and democracy, but oversharing erases the public/private boundary that is necessary for good mental and emotional health.

Sharing has become a verb, meaning "to tell." I share my personal information, tastes in food, gossip. Sharing is good; it tethers people together (Turkle 2011). The enormous upside of the Internet and smartphones is that people can share anytime, anywhere. We are connected to the many **contacts** we have on our phones, Facebook, Twitter. Turkle argues persuasively that these are weak ties in the sense that we no longer have an obligation to each other imposed on us by face-to-face interaction, and we can acquire and shed relationships too easily. Internet dating is an example of this: The person returns from a date and goes online immediately to find a better dating partner. Phoning and texting are also examples; we can ignore people, creating a generalized anxiety that requires us to attend to these devices compulsively, hoping that we won't be ignored.

Sending messages to each other is a way of sending the self, signaling one's cosmic position and leaving a trail. As I have noted, these messages need not be weighty, and they may be emoticon- and slang-ridden. I suppose that the Platonic dialogues could have been texted, but, more likely, teenagers are using it to gossip about relationships, music, school, and their parents.

I am concerned here about the psychological implications of sending the self into cyberspace, of oversharing by another name. And, as I argued, texting and emailing are only two vehicles of this. Others are social media, dating sites, and pornography. All launch the self into cyberspace, hoping for connection. But all of this can be unhealthy emotionally for the person, who risks losing herself by laying herself bare. That is the peril of a pornographic public sphere in which there are no secrets, but also in which nothing important is being said. The theorist Theodor Adorno (1973) termed this the **jargon of authenticity**, chattering about everyday life in a way that trivializes everything.

Community, not Connection

In telephone talk, connection refers to making successful phone contact with another person. It has become a dating term—"we have a connection." This means that there is something between us, affection, emotion, perhaps potentially love. It is easy to connect electronically, by emailing, Facebooking, texting, tweeting, using online dating, webcamming sexually. We can be at home, work or Starbucks as we connect using our phones and laptops.

I contend that these connections are flimsy and largely unfulfilling as people are, in Turkle's words, "alone together." We spend much of our days now signaling our position in the world and trading notes with our contacts and FB friends. This is thin, not thick, for two reasons: Few words are actually exchanged, and we can ignore the last message, effectively cutting off communication. Everyone knows the experience of sending a message, getting nothing in return, and wondering where she stands with the other person. This breeds insecurity and anxiety, which, when mixed with prior abuse and emotional distance, can reinforce serious psychological problems, such as the personality disorders discussed earlier.

The curious thing about these electronic connections is that people seem to divulge so much about themselves and thus make way for real intimacy. But self-revelation, without the sense of obligation and reciprocity found in voice-to-voice and face-to-face speech and old-fashioned letter writing, is exhibitionism, the narcissistic cry for help: "Look at me! I had enchiladas for dinner. I had a margarita. I got drunk. I had casual sex." The connection between low self-esteem and narcissism is this: No one else will love me and so I will love myself, or at least objectify myself, like Narcissus, by gazing at my reflection in the mirror or, now, in pornographic videos. A pornographic culture is a culture of self-exposers, of people who watch themselves—what earlier I called leaving a trail. Facebook is the perfect vehicle for this because we can track our own postings, which appear, objectified, on the screen, as do our photos and the photos of our friends—proving to ourselves that we have friends, even if only Facebook friends and the contacts on our phones.

I am reading compulsive self-revelation as an attempt to find love, if, initially, only self-love. Like the message in a bottle cast out to sea, occasionally one's self-revelation finds a connection, which could become real community. The difference between **connection** and **community** is that the former is only contact, an acknowledgement of one's existence. You had enchiladas for dinner; I hear you. You sleep around; I think that is hot. Community is not only acknowledgment but reciprocity based on dialogue. By **reciprocity** I mean the obligation to the other speaker or writer, the other self, to continue dialogue, to build a real relationship.

This can be done online; the old term for this is pen pals. Distance shrinks in an era of global connectivity, which is a good thing. I in Texas can have a friend in Maine, or even China. Everyone knows a story of pen pals who think they have fallen in love, finally meet and consummate their love. I know an American woman who formed a relationship with a guy in Sweden this way. It can work. Thus, I want to be hesitant about viewing online and offline communication as entirely different. There is a boundary between them that can be crossed. Offline and online interaction can enrich each other as long as the latter does not replace the former.

People with low self-esteem venture little and expect less. "Friending" someone in Facebook terminology is not like asking someone out on a date, although being ignored stings. One can rationalize being ignored: They never got my request; they don't log on often. Although high-school lovers may expect their paramour to text back almost immediately, adults realize that people are busy and may ignore or overlook the many texts sent to them. They may take the same attitude toward email, although ignoring someone is rude, especially when email resembles traditional letters more than does texting, which is like a Post-It note with emoticons and acronyms.

The neo-Freudian Karen Horney (1937) talked about the neurotic personality of our time. People are still neurotic (I just raised my hand, but you couldn't see me!), but I am concerned that emotional problems have deepened, and low self-esteem has mired people in full-fledged personality disorders. The neurotic is anxious, but the borderline person combines impulsivity with a compulsive need for connection, from which she then backs off in a self-defeating way. The borderline person cannot stand being alone, for which texting is tailor-made. Armed with our phones, a connection is a few keystrokes away.

As for the narcissist, Facebook and Twitter are the vehicles of choice. We can scream our opinions and accomplishments to the world, thus at least pleasing ourselves, as we examine our FB "walls" and discover that we have left a trail and even provoked a few people to "like" what we have said and "comment" on it. This form of oversharing makes me want to look away, even more than pornographic sites and dating sites on which men post photos of their erect penises. It is painful to listen to people on FB crowing about their cooking, their brilliant children, how they will make great professors. Even when they don't brag, they post sheer trivia about their days and their views. Facebook and Twitter overlap in this sense, although Facebook is also driven by photographs.

The sociologist Mark Worrell (2011) comments on the pathology of being ignored:

> I think that oversharing is found to be necessary by people who do not want to be ignored. Almost every post on Facebook, etc., is generally ignored. Hitting the "Like" button on a post is a way of pretending that you're paying attention while not paying attention at all—this can be added to the list … as a reason to "like" something: I'm pretending not to ignore you as I ignore you. I ran an experiment last year where I posted a link to a song and people "Liked" it and made comments and then later I posted a link to a "song" that, as it turns out, was 30 seconds of silence. I got the same quantity of "Like" and banal comments as the actual song

from, pretty much, the same set of folks. One would have to be, not a narcissist, but an altruist (self-less) to endure this. Real narcissists and egoists run screaming from F-Book or go into those borderline fits of love and hate. I think F-Book can even trigger borderline-like reactions from normal people looking for substantive online interactions: well, if you're only going to pretend to pay attention then so long. Going too far and making a spectacle of one's self is one way that a person can evade being ignored.

Philosophy, once a considered outcome of people's literary imagination, is now written in units of the "tweet," a Twitter text byte. It is perhaps understandable that we might like to know what the famous movie star or athlete had for Thanksgiving dinner, but no one wants to know what you and I ate.

The Martian anthropologist would find this endemic narcissism pathetic. On Mars, there is no Facebook, and no ego screaming. There is no psychotherapy on Mars because Martians, peculiarly, all have high self-esteem, probably feeling themselves superior to fragile earthlings!

A Non-Pornographic Culture

Pornography is not the main problem. It is simply a metaphor for a society in which people bare all, hoping to feel better about themselves and to connect. But oversharing rarely accomplishes its desired end: love, intimacy, community. It merely positions the person, usually electronically, in a chatty world in which people possibly gossip and share opinions, ungrounded in systematic study. This has two negative effects: It impoverishes public discourse, reducing it to tweets and blogs. And it triggers personality disorders based in narcissistic grandiosity, impulsivity, and love–hate relationships.

It is no wonder that people's interior lives would be so violated by our pornographic culture. There are fewer boundaries than ever today. When I was young, the world couldn't penetrate the walls of our house or my psychic interior except via television, which was only network and featured cartoons on Saturday, the afternoon baseball game and situation comedies. The rest of the time we would be outside playing, inventing games, and doing sports without the oversight of **helicopter parents**, a category which didn't exist. I grew up in an academic household and my parents scarcely ever checked my homework, or even asked whether I had completed it. The pressure was much less than kids face today, as they live accelerated, adult-like lives way before their time.

My own kids may own iPhones and have many contacts and FB friends. They even have a lot of real friends. But they are burdened—by pornography, sex, homework, the lack of downtime—in ways that I never was. And I was worldly, having traveled to Europe. But I had an early bedtime, wandered my neighborhood safely, and didn't face temptation at every turn.

What can we do to mitigate the effects of this see-all, say-all world in which we live? Here are some ideas, all of which begin with individual choice.

- People can start their kids on cellphones and the Internet when they are well into their teenage years.
- Kids need bedtimes after which they can't text or surf.
- Parents should check their kids' cells for sexting.
- Parents should keep an eye on their kids' Facebook pages.
- Adults, especially men, should rethink the role of pornography in their lives. They can bring their fantasies into their own relationships, where they are no longer fantasies but just ways of being sexual in committed relationships.
- People should try to meet potential partners in the normal course of their lives, including at work, instead of relying on online dating, which resembles a meat-market and discourages real commitment. Online daters move from date to date, relationship to relationship, like people putting on and taking off clothes in a store dressing room.
- People should limit their use of their smartphones—texting, emailing, surfing. We are rapidly becoming a country in which people inhabit the same physical space but are isolated as they work their phones. As Turkle says, they are "alone together."
- Replace texting and emailing with talking on the phone and meeting in person.
- Parents should insist that kids call instead of text, developing good social skills.
- Facebook is useful for catching up with friends distant in time and space, sharing stories and photos. But it is a petri dish of narcissism, and people should unplug from it. Secretly, we all know that it is boring, but, like many addictions, we cannot live without it.
- We should resign from Twitter because tweeting our every location, activity and random thought is pathetic and dumbs down the culture.
- We should attempt to preserve privacy by avoiding oversharing in all of these and other ways.

When we are happy with ourselves, we won't crave exhibition and connection, especially of the electronic varieties. Being happy with ourselves involves more than a dose of self-esteem. It involves work that we enjoy and love—Freud's basic recipe. Simply turning off our phones won't change the world, but it will be a step toward allowing us to recoup, regaining the time and space in which we can be human and really think through our issues. Reining in our penchant for texting, tweeting, and Facebooking requires self-discipline. Having other activities, including work and intimate relationships, helps divert us from the time sink of endless electronic connection, which fills a gap. Cooper (2011) urges breaks or "fasts" from the electronic media in his self-published book *Fast Media, Media Fast*.

Anyone who "uses"—a drug-addiction term for habitual consumers of drugs—knows that these electronic connections are enticing, and the user quickly becomes compulsive about checking and deploying them. One solution is not to possess the technology in the first place; a phone that cannot text ensures that one will never get sucked into endless exchanges. But that seems overly self-sacrificing; I just inherited my son's BlackBerry, after a few years of owning a stupidphone (as I call it). He traded up to an iPhone. I have trouble with the BlackBerry because the keys seem tiny, but, then again, I mainly use the phone for phone calls and the occasional text to my kids or one of their tennis-playing friends. And I sometimes text during boring work meetings (a tautology, that!), just to break up the tedium. I get the feeling that I am violating etiquette because few of my other colleagues engage in this adolescent behavior.

One can use technology without being used by it, a central insight of Herbert Marcuse, one of the original members of the Frankfurt School of critical theorists. Marcuse (1969) speculated about a new technology that would play with nature and express our creative purposes. His younger colleague, Jurgen Habermas (1971), disagrees with him that we can "pacify" technology. For Habermas, technology will always impose its will on us, requiring us to be deliberate and rational in the ways we debate the uses of technology (see Agger 1976).

I agree with both of them. We can transform work on nature into a creative and self-expressive activity; imagine gardening and raising vegetables. In this book series, Kevin Wehr (2012) considers the do-it-yourself movement. But some technologies compel us to behave in self-destructive ways. Think of automobiles hurtling down a highway with their drivers in their own private spheres, unconnected to the world. And think of smartphones that are always beeping and buzzing with other people's messages and texts and, occasionally, calls.

We cannot leave capitalism out of the equation here. Phone companies and Internet service providers charge expensive monthly fees for service plans and access. And phones and computers are themselves a big business. People view these charges as necessities in a world in which everyone seems to text and surf, much as they view cable television (or a satellite dish) as a necessity. I was totally content for years without any cellphone, and then with a stupidphone. I inherited cast-off phones from my kids, and was placed on an already-existing family plan.

As capitalism shifted from an ethic of saving (Adam Smith, Luther, Calvin) to an ethic of spending (post-World War II, Keynes), aided by credit buying, advertising was called on to create needs where none may have existed before (see Ewen 1976; Leiss 1976). Even an hour spent watching television will reveal the hard sell put on by cellphone companies. 4G is supposedly better than 3G, and iPhones superior to Droids. Phone- and Internet-related advertisements dominate the airwaves, rivaled, in off hours, by ads for medicines such as Viagra that address erectile dysfunction.

In this environment, it is no wonder that everyone wants and buys a smartphone, with its expensive monthly plan. We are now awash in **apps**, an Apple word for applications but now used by other telephone platforms. An app is something we can click on that will give us the latest sports scores, provide us with restaurant reviews, and allow us to play video games. Many apps cost money, another revenue stream for the insatiable phone companies. Teenagers can't be cool without a phone equipped with many apps.

Information, entertainment, and communication technologies are defined by capitalism, which wants to turn a profit. There is no Technology, with a capitalized first letter, that is a demonic deux ex machina—with a mind and purpose of its own. There are only uses of technologies, applications if you will. I am not suggesting that in my utopia there would be no phones, email, even texting. I don't care if people use texting to arrange their lives pragmatically. I do care that texting, tweeting, and Facebooking are dumbing down the culture and exacerbating personality disorders as people screech and scream about their lives, all the while feeling wholly inadequate. A friend of my son observed that, "No one puts their phone down," meaning that it has become a prosthetic extension of themselves. Capitalism wants it no other way, as phone and computer companies make billions from people who have been brainwashed to believe that the 4G iPhone is The Next Big Thing, without which they cannot be happy.

Yes, I am saying that oversharing and capitalism are related to each other. Capitalism beats us down by making us feel small in our work lives, and families tend not to provide us with the self-esteem necessary to find and form solid personal relationships. And then capitalism profits from communication technologies that allow us to overshare, seeking to leave our mark on a world that doesn't particularly welcome us. We say too much and we use a dumbed-down discourse of LOL and emoticons, thus creating a culture in which all are naked, on display for everyone else. We do not derive satisfaction from this, but we keep busy communicating, surfing, using our apps. And we spend our money.

It is well and good to suggest that we should change capitalism and families. I am saying nothing less than that we should. But, meantime, the person can begin to change her own life, choosing work that is fulfilling, forming relationships and families in which people are nurtured and not beaten down, and finding ways of revealing oneself and building community that are not pornographic. We will keep some mystery in our lives, refusing to tell all. We will keep our personal lives personal, and yet we will form community with like-minded friends. We will all be healthier and happier for tuning out and turning off the technologies of oversharing. Only then can we begin really to share—to be intimate, to love, and to open ourselves to love.

References

Adorno, Theodor W. 1954. "How to Look at Television." *Quarterly of Film, Radio and Television* 3: 213–35.

———. 1973. *The Jargon of Authenticity*. Evanston, IL: Northwestern University Press.

Agger, Ben. 1976. "Marcuse and Habermas on New Science." *Polity* 9, 2: 158–81.

———. 1990. *Decline of Discourse: Reading, Writing and Resistance in Postmodern Capitalism*. London: Falmer.

———. 2011a. *Body Problems: Running and Living Long in a Fast-Food Society*. New York: Routledge.

———. 2011b. "iTime: Labor and Life in the Smartphone Era." *Time and Society* 20, 1: 119–36.

Agger, Ben and Beth Anne Shelton. 2007. *Fast Families, Virtual Children: A Critical Sociology of Families and Schooling*. Boulder: Paradigm.

Alford, Henry. 2011. "Is Anyone There?" *New York Times* (July 15).

American Psychiatric Association. 2000. *Diagnostic and Statistical Manual of Mental Disorders IV-TR*. Washington, D.C.: American Psychiatric Association.

Begley, Sharon. 2011. "I Can't Think." *Newsweek* (March 2).

Bourdieu, Pierre. 1986. "The Forms of Capital." Pp. 241–58 in *Handbook for Theory and Research for the Sociology of Education*, ed. J. G. Richardson. New York: Greenwood Press.

Brashears, Matthew E. Forthcoming. "Small Networks and High Isolation? A Reexamination of American Discussion Networks. *Social Networks*.

Chua, Amy. 2011. *Battle Hymn of the Tiger Mother*. New York: Penguin.

Cooper, Thomas. 2011. *Fast Media, Media Fast*. Bloomington, IN: AuthorHouse.

Cotten, Shelia R., Melinda Goldner, Timothy M. Hale, and Patricia Dentrea. 2011. "The Importance of Type, Amount and Timing of Internet for Understanding Psychological Distress." *Social Science Quarterly* 92, 1: 119–39.

Debord, Guy. 1983. *Society of the Spectacle*. Detroit: Black & Red.

Dershowitz, Alan M. 1998. *Sexual McCarthyism: Clinton, Starr, and the Emerging Constitutional Crisis*. New York: Basic.

Durkheim, Emile. 1950. *Rules of Sociological Method*. Glencoe, IL: Free Press.

———. 1951. *Suicide: A Study in Sociology*. Glencoe, IL: Free Press.

Ewen, Stewart. 1976. *Captains of Consciousness: Advertising and the Social Roots of the Consumer Culture*. New York: McGraw-Hill.

Freud, Sigmund. 1991. *The Interpretation of Dreams*. Oxford: Oxford University Press.

Goffman, Erving. 1959. *The Presentation of Self in Everyday Life*. New York: Doubleday.

———. 1974. *Frame Analysis: An Essay on the Organization of Experience*. New York: Harper and Row.

Goodale, Gloria. 2010. Personal Correspondence.

Gould, Emily. 2008. "Exposed." *New York Times Magazine* (May 25).

———. 2010. *And the Heart Says Whatever*. New York: Free Press.

Habermas, Jurgen. 1971. *Toward a Rational Society*. Boston: Beacon.

———. 1984. *The Theory of Communicative Action*. Vol. 1. Boston: Beacon.

———. 1987. *The Theory of Communicative Action*. Vol. 2. Boston: Beacon.

Hegel, G. W. F. 1967. *The Phenomenology of Mind*. New York: Harper and Row.

Hill, D. W. 2009. "Reflections on Leaving Facebook." *Fast Capitalism* 5, 2.

Horney, Karen. 1937. *The Neurotic Personality of Our Time*. New York: Norton.

Jacobs, Gloria E. 2006. "Fast Times and Digital Literacy: Participation Roles and Portfolio Construction within Instant Messaging." *Journal of Literacy Research* 38, 2: 171–96.

———. 2008. "Saying Something or Having Something to Say: Attention Seeking, the Breakdown of Privacy, and the Promise of Discourse in the Blogosphere." *Fast Capitalism* 4, 1.

———. 2009. *Adolescents and Instant Messaging: Literacy, Language, and Identity Development in the 21st Century*. Saarbrücken: VDM Verlag.

Jacoby, Russell. 1976. "A Falling Rate of Intelligence?" *Telos* 27: 141–46.

Lasch, Christopher. 1979. *The Culture of Narcissism*. New York: Norton.

Laumann, Edward O., John H. Gagnon, Robert T. Michael and Stuart Michaels. 1994. *The Social Organization of Sexuality: Sexual Practices in the United States*. Chicago: University of Chicago Press.

Lee, Patty. 2010. "Thirty Percent of Women, 70 Percent of Men Confess to Looking at Online Porn: Study." *New York Daily News* (February 11) (http://articles.nydailynews.com/2010-02-11/entertainment/27056038_1_study-big-issue-problem—retrieved October 3, 2011).

Leiss, William. 1976. *The Limits to Satisfaction: An Essay on the Problem of Needs and Commodities*. Toronto: University of Toronto Press.

Lowe, Pam K., Simon J. Williams, and Frances Griffiths. 2007. "Embodying and Embedding Children's Sleep: Sociological Comments and Observations." *Sociological Research Online* 12, 5 (http://www.socresonline.org.uk/12/5/6.html—retrieved October 3, 2011).

McGuigan, Jim. 2005. "Towards a Sociology of the Mobile Phone." *Human Technology* 1, 1: 45–57.

Marcuse, Herbert. 1955. *Eros and Civilization*. New York: Vintage.

———. 1969. *An Essay on Liberation*. Boston: Beacon.

Maslow, Abraham. 1970. *Motivation and Personality*, 2nd ed. New York: Harper & Row.

Mill, John Stuart. 2003. *On Liberty*. New Haven: Yale University Press.

Miller, Mark Crispin. 1988. *Boxed In: The Culture of TV*. Evanston, IL: Northwestern University Press.

Pew Research Center. 2011. "Teen and Young Adult Internet Use." http://pewresearch.org/millennials/teen-internet-use-graphic.php.

Rippin, Hannah. 2005. "The Mobile Phone in Everyday Life." 1.1 *Fast Capitalism*. www.fastcapitalism.com.

Salinger, J. D. 1951. *The Catcher in the Rye*. Boston: Little, Brown.

Smith, T. C. and S. P. Novella. 2007. "HIV Denial in the Internet Era." *PLoS Med* 4, 8: e256. doi:10.1371/journal.pmed.0040256.

Thompson, Clive. 2008. "The Brave New World of Digital Intimacy." *New York Times* (September 5).

Turkle, Sherry. 1995. *Life on the Screen: Identity in the Age of the Internet.* New York: Simon & Schuster.

———. 2011. *Alone Together: Why We Expect more from Technology and Less from Each Other.* New York: Basic.

UPI (United Press International). 2009. "Sociologist: Few Teens 'Sexting'" (January 11) (http://www.upi.com/Top_News/2009/01/11/Sociologist-Few-teens-sexting/UPI-78141231654189/—retrieved October 3, 2011).

Vitzthum, Virginia. 2007. *I Love You, Let's Meet: Adventures in Online Dating.* Boston: Little, Brown.

Wehr, Kevin. 2012. *Do it Yourself: The Search for Control and Self-Reliance in the 21st Century.* New York: Routledge.

Worrell, Mark. 2011. Personal correspondence.

Žižek, Slavoj. 2005. Interview with Wolfgang Tillmans. *Index Magazine* (http://www.indexmagazine.com/interviews/slavoj_zizek.shtml—retrieved October 3, 2011).

———. 2006. *The Pervert's Guide to Cinema.* DVD. Memorable Quotes (http://www.imdb.com/title/tt0828154/quotes—retrieved October 3, 2011).

Glossary/Index

A

Adorno, Theodor xi, 44

Agger, Ben 6, 8, 16, 22, 49

Alford, Henry 12

alienation: Marx's term for being out of control of one's life, especially because one is merely an employee of big business 16

amateur porn: pornography depicting regular people, not paid actors, having sex 18, 37, 38, 39, 40, 41

American Psychiatric Association 6

And the Heart Said Whatever 2

anomie: Durkheim's term for being alone in a crowd, untethered by strong social ties 18

apps: short for applications, software that can be run on a phone or computer, originating from iPhone discourse 50

Ashley Madison 29

B

banality, immersion in 3, 4, 7

BBW: dating lingo for big beautiful woman 30

Begley, Sharon 2

bi-curious: a straight (heterosexual) person curious about having sex with someone of one's own gender 37

blogging 2, 11, 12, 47

bodies; erection photographs 33–4, 37, 40; images of sexualized 34; problems 6–7; shaved genital area 32, 34, 39; through a pornographic prism 41, 42; trafficking in 6, 32–3, 34

bondage: tying up or restraining one's sexual partner during sex, typically with the man restraining the woman 18, 33, 39

borderline personality disorder: a serious emotional disturbance characterized by impulsive behavior and love-hate relationships, possibly stemming from earlier abuse 6, 7, 13, 46, 47

Bourdieu, Pierre 22
breasts 34

C

capitalism 49–50

Catcher in the Rye 37

celebrities 2, 4–5, 17

Chatroulette 18

chatting: breezy conversations sometimes conducted online via instant messaging 25

Chua, Amy 15

commercialization of love and sex: putting a price on dating and intimate physical relationships, such as via online dating services, pay-for-view pornography and prostitution 29

communication, online and offline 26–7, 46

community: real people who share certain values and interact frequently, whether face-to-face, online or both 45; adolescent forming of 8, 14; not connection 45–7; searching for 3–4, 8; texting as 13

concealment 3, 5, 12–13

connection: less substantial relationships that are often here today and gone tomorrow (by contrast to community, which is more enduring) 45; addictive nature of 48–9; community not 45–7; searching for 3–4, 8, 12–13

contacts: people with whom one is regularly in electronic contact, such as phone friends 13, 44, 45

Cooper, Thomas 49

Cotten, Sheila 25

cougar: older, more sexually experienced woman 30

cracking: allows an app to run on a phone for free 16

Craigslist 24, 33, 34

cyberdemocracy: democratic institutions and practices such as voting and debate conducted online 22

D

deboundarying: a postmodern term for erasing distinctions between public and private life such as work and family 3

decline of discourse: my term for the dilution of public debate and discussion in favor of chatting and gossip about a star culture and other everyday matters 22–6

Dershowitz, Alan 37

Diagnostic and Statistical Manual of Mental Disorders DSM-IV-TR 6

Digital Youth Research Project 3

discourse: the ways in which people talk and write about the world 24

domination/submission: the man pulls the woman's hair and spanks her as the woman subordinates herself to the male's desire 18, 33, 38–9, 40, 43

drama: interpersonal intrigue often given momentum by texting and blogging 5, 8, 26

Durkheim, Emile 6, 16

E

email 2, 12, 17, 27, 40, 46, 48

erectile dysfunction (ED) 34

erection photographs 33–4, 37, 40

Eros and Civilization 43

exhibitionism 4–5, 17, 18, 23, 40, 45

extramarital affairs 31–2

F

face-to-face vs. online communication 13–14, 26–7

Facebook 2; being ignored on 46–7; friends on 2, 3–4, 20, 26, 46; likes and comments on 22, 25, 46–7; and narcissism 46; as the new television 20–2; postings on 20, 22, 25; relationship status on 14; unplugging from 20, 48

falling rate of intelligence: Russell Jacoby's term for what I call the decline of discourse. People know more about Hollywood stars and less about what happened during World War II, for example 23

false consciousness: Marx's term for people not knowing their best interests and needs, provoked by ideologies that deceive them 39

fast capitalism: my term for an Internet-based capitalism in which buying, selling, and advertising often occur online and 24/7, without relief. Postmodern capitalism is a synonym for this. 8

Fast Media, Media Fast 49

framing: the way in which people construct online dating profiles to emphasize their strengths and mute their weaknesses 28–9, 31–3

Freud, Sigmund 5, 43, 48

to friend: a Facebook term for inviting someone to be on one's list of people who have access to one's wall 3–4

G

gender roles: the ways in which we are taught to be feminine and masculine - e.g., keeping house and playing sports 29–31, 40

gender socialization: the many ways in which we are taught, by family, peers and our culture, to learn gender roles 32

Goffman, Erving 1, 28

K

kinky: a socially- and culturally-relative term for sexual behavior that is somewhat outside the lines of heterosexual normalcy; often depicted in pornography. 18, 33, 34, 36–7, 42

knowledge: as opposed to mere information, more substantial understanding of the world, such as what makes people happy and what is just and fair 24–5, 26

L

Lasch, Christopher 3

Laumann, Edward 32

Lee, Patty 36

life instinct: Herbert Marcuse's term for Freud's notion of Eros, which emphasizes that people have an instinctual basis for seeking love, community, freedom from oppression 43

Lowe, Pam 15

LTR: internet dating lingo for long-term relationship 32

Lyman, Peter 3

M

Marcuse, Herbert 43, 49

marketplace of ideas: John Stuart Mill's term for the way in which ideas are thrown out into the public sphere and the strongest survive 23

Markoff, Philip 33

Maslow, Abraham 9

McGuigan, Jim 2

MILF: dating lingo for mother I'd like to … (use your imagination!) 30

Mill, John Stuart 23

Miller, Mark Crispin xi

Modern Family 21

N

narcissism 4, 8, 45, 46, 47

narcissistic personality disorder (NPD): a serious emotional disorder involving the belief that the person knows best for everyone else and has no flaws 6, 7, 47

neurotic personalities 46

newspapers 23–4

non-pornographic public sphere: a public world in which we don't lay everything bare but preserve the boundary between public and private life 17, 18, 23, 44–50; community not connection 45–7; and non-pornographic culture 47–50

Novella, S.P. 24

NSA: dating lingo for a no-strings-attached relationship 30

O

Obama, Barack 20, 23

online dating 28–35, 48; gendered nature of 29–31; and marital status 31–2; over-sharing in 28, 30

photographs as text of 30, 32–3, 33–4, 37

self-framing 28–9, 31–3

opinion 22–3, 24–5, 25–6

oversharing: Emily Gould's term for telling too much about oneself, often online and through texting and blogging xi–xii, 2, 12, 14, 18, 46, 47; blurring of boundaries 1–3, 26–7; and capitalism 50; features of 3–5; and online dating 28, 30; in online vs. face-to-face communication 13–14, 26–7; pornography and 36; psychiatry of 6–9; ways to avoid 48–9

P

Pascoe, C.J. 17

personality disorders 6–9, 13, 46, 47

phone calls 11, 12–13, 44, 45

phone companies 49–50

playing: the activities of an insincere dater, often a male, who is not serious about relationships 5

pornographic prism: the way in which we view and construct our own sexuality by watching porn actors 40–2, 43

pornographic public sphere: a public world in which every aspect of personal or private life is made visible 17, 26, 38, 43, 44

pornography: the depiction, often onscreen and online, of people having sex xi, 8, 36–43; and obsession with sex 42–3; and pornographic prism 40–2, 43; videos 36–9

post-textual age: an era when people, especially post-baby boomers, learn much about the world from images, photos, videos and music 25

The Presentation of Self in Everyday Life 1

prison code: the ways in which kids secretly talk amongst themselves, especially at night, when adults are asleep, primarily using texting 14–15

professional porn: porn depicting paid actors 37–8, 41

public discourse: the ways in which people in the public sphere talk about major issues such as politics, the economy and culture 22, 47

public sphere: Habermas' term for the world outside of the home and family 9

Q

Quotidian events: everyday occurrences 3, 4, 8, 20, 22

R

Reciprocity: an interaction style in which both parties care for the well-being and feelings of the other person 12, 45

repression, sexual and religious 17, 37, 38

Rippin, Hannah 2

Role playing: sexual scenarios where people pretend to be someone other than who they are (e.g., cheerleader) 37

S

Salinger, J.D. 37

self-esteem, low 6, 7, 45, 46

Serendipity: when things seem to happen accidentally, but with good results 31

Sex addict: supposedly, some people obsess about sex in the way that alcoholics become addicted to drink 38

Sex drive: the impulse, identified by Freud, to have sex, an impulse that he felt was central to human nature 43

Sexting: sending sexy or pornographic text messages, including photos 17–18, 27, 33

Sexual libertarianism: the attitude that almost 'anything goes' between consenting adults 37

Sexual McCarthyism: a Puritanical political agenda that places a taboo on non-traditional sexual practices 37

Sexualization: a tendency for everyday life to be dominated by sexuality, including the display of the sexual body 43

Sexualized culture: a public world dominated by porn and open discourse about sexuality 33, 34

Sharing: a contemporary word for trading or telling secrets 3, 44

shaved genital area 32, 34, 39

Shelton, Anne 16

Skype 18

sleep deprivation 15

Smartphones 2, 15, 21, 25, 48, 50

Smith, T.C. 24

social media 5, 6, 18, 20–7

and decline of discourse 22–6

online vs. offline communication 26–7

Social Network 20

Spinning: a tendency to lie or shade the truth to one's own advantage 5

Stigma: a negative label attached to a forbidden or discouraged activity 18

Stress: a feeling of being trapped in one's own life, with too much to do and too little time to do it 16, 34

SWF: a dating term for single white female 30

Swinging: when people have multiple sexual partners, often trading spouses. Swingers separate love and sex 18, 33

Symbolic interactionism: a sociological perspective, owed to Mead, that emphasizes people's interactions and the meanings they attach to these interactions 1

T

teenagers; measures to avoid oversharing 48–9; in pre Internet era 8, 13, 14–15, 37, 47, 48; pressures on contemporary 16, 47–8; prison code of 14, 17; relationship with parents 15; sexting 17, 18; texting 8, 11–12, 13, 14–15, 16–17, 44; and understanding of sexual experimentation 42; vampirization of 15, 16; writing 8

texting 13, 16, 25, 46, 49; and being ignored 44, 45, 46; positioning self through 11–14; teenage 11–12, 13, 14–15, 16–17, 44; writing messages 8, 11, 12, 27

thin boundaries: a psychological term for the tendency to be influenced by other people that accompanies the loss of a stable self-identity 7

Thompson, Clive 22

tiger mothers 15, 16

TMI: a contemporary acronym for too much information 4, 5, 8

trail, leaving a 11–14, 22, 44, 46

Turkle, Sherry 15, 16, 44

tweeting 11–12, 13, 14, 21, 25, 47, 48, 50

Twitter 2, 46, 47, 48

V

vampirization 15, 16

Vitzthum, Virginia 28

voyeurism 4–5, 17, 18, 21

vulnerability 13

W

web cams 17, 18, 27, 38

Wikipedia 23, 24

window period: the period of early infection by the HIV virus before antibodies show up in tests, usually thought to be between 6 and 8 weeks 24

Worrell, Mark 21, 46

writing 2, 25; adolescent 8; on online dating sites 30; oversharing in 13–14; texts 8, 11, 12, 27

Y

youporn.com 36–7

Z

Žižek, Slavoj 41